MW00330172

A Journey into the Heart

of the Black Madonna

A Journey into the Heart of the Black Madonna

Self-Discovery, Spiritualism, Activism

CINDY M. MEDINA

A Journey into the Heart of the Black Madonna:

Self-Discovery, Spiritualism, Activism

Copyright ©2016 Cindy M. Medina

ISBN: 978-1-940769-60-8

Publisher: Mercury HeartLink

Printed in the United States of America

No part of this eBook may be reproduced or transmitted in any form or by any means, electronic or mechanical, including photocopying, recording or by any information storage and retrieval system, without written permission from the author.

Some names and identifying details have been changed to protect the privacy of individuals.

The author has made every effort to ensure the accuracy of the information within this book was correct at time of publication. The author does not assume and hereby disclaims any liability to any party for any loss, damage, or disruption caused by errors or omissions, whether such errors or omissions result from accident, negligence, or any other cause.

Contact the author: *dreams@cindymmedina.com*

Mercury HeartLink
www.heartlink.com

A Journey into the Heart of the Black Madonna

Acknowledgments

A million thanks to my publisher Stewart S. Warren at Mercury HeartLink, copy editor Cinny Green, editor Charlie McKee, proofreader Trina Rivera, and website designer Marissa Cyrus. With deep gratitude for support from Dr. Russell A. Lockhart, my loving family, my dearest friends, the Dream Group, the Sophia's Writers Circle, and my writing mentors who offered their encouragement on my writer's journey.

ೞ   ೞ   ೞ

View the image of the Black Madonna of Einsiedeln, as well as other inspirational images, on *www.cindymmedina.com*.

ೞ   ೞ   ೞ

Front cover is an original painting used with permission by the artist, Lindsey Leavell, *www.lindseyleavell.com*. Her paintings are represented by Abbey Lane Gallery in Creede, Colorado.

DEDICATION

For men and women who are longing
for a loving and compassionate presence
in their daily life, may the Black
Madonna help you to discover your
spiritual and psychological legacy.

For my grandchildren, Carolina and
Lukas, and my nephews, Pablito and
Jake, who symbolize the Divine Child in
all of us.

A Journey into the Heart

of the Black Madonna

PREFACE

While watching the news on television, I saw a clip that a statue of the Virgin Mary was beheaded, and her hands were severed in a Catholic Church in the United States. I was horrified by this picture. Who was destroying this universal symbol of love and acceptance? When I read newspapers, I cringed at the bloody violence that was pulverizing families and communities in America. A common thread was: "The mass killer was a loner." "He didn't have many friends." "He spent a lot of time on the computer." I asked myself: *Psychologically, what makes the loner so violent? What does the computer contain that he spends hours searching for it? Is he trying to belong to some cause or a relationship where he would feel accepted? Is he gathering information on ways to destroy, or is this his desperate attempt to connect with someone?* Whether it was killings inspired by the Islamic State, the high rate of suicide among teenagers, or the high death rate caused by heroin and other drugs, I felt that the world was collapsing.

All my questions led me to the conclusion that compassion was required to help alleviate violence and to bring personal and societal healing. What greater symbol for compassion than the Black Madonna? Could I share my journey with men and women in the form of a book to remind them of this archetype and her psychic resources?

But when I thought about writing a book, I rejected this idea. Writing was never my forte, and I refused to share my relationship with the Black Madonna with a wider audience. I felt comfortable speaking with a limited audience at conferences and talking about the unconscious during dream workshops, but a book was different. After my encounter with this Feminine archetype, I reconnected with different aspects of myself, like meeting a great-grandmother whom I had forgotten. The Black Madonna had become my secret as if she were my favorite fishing hole. What if people judged my relationship with her that now was sealed with mutual love?

However, the more I saw how people suffered from isolation, emotional and physical abandonment, and loneliness, the more I was convinced that now is the time to reacquaint men and women with the maternal aspects of their psyche. I wanted them to know that, no matter what situation unfolded, they would find solutions in this maternal presence of love. In this process, their true potentials would be revealed.

The more I became involved in social activism, the more clearly I saw with the eyes of my heart the environmental destruction in the world. I became aware of polluted rivers, streams, oceans, and bays that families depended on for their livelihood—waterways that were being filled with everything imaginable from raw stinky sewage to heavy metals and trash to hazardous chemicals—as if these waterways were a dumpster. Most people who are reading this preface are not poisoning the waterways, but they may know someone—a neighbor, an acquaintance, or an employer—who is. What will help you, the reader, be courageous enough to bring justice to this environmental tragedy? I believe men and women can find their source of courage in the dark recesses of the Feminine lying within their psyches.

One example of courage began on August 15, 1928, the Feast of the Assumption, when Agnes Gonxha Bojaxhiu traveled as a pilgrim to southeast Kosovo for the Feast of the Black Madonna of Vitina-Letnica. While praying to the Black Madonna, she received confirmation of her calling to be a missionary nun. Later, Agnes became Mother Teresa of Calcutta who founded the Missionaries of Charity and served the dying of Calcutta. As she searched for a home for the suffering, the City of Calcutta offered her the abandoned Hindu Temple Kali, a temple to a goddess who was over two thousand years old, dating back to the pre-Aryan Great Mother Goddess. This goddess was revered by Hindus as Mother Kali, most compassionate and of incomprehensible love.

While some Hindus protested against Mother Teresa, a white Christian woman, using their goddess's temple, the municipality defended Mother Teresa's work. She continued using the restored Kali temple for hospice care.

I thought this abandoned Kali temple was a perfect place for Hindus, Christians, Muslims, and others to receive love and dignity during the final days of their lives! The images of the Black Madonna, the goddess Kali, and the Great Mother Goddess all represent the divine manifestation of God. Mother Teresa's works were an example of the Feminine's love-in-action. A call to action is required in these turbulent times. The Feminine is here to help with her values of intuition, the need for relationships that instill a sense of belonging and emotional closeness, and a maternal aspect of compassion to a world that is imploding from violence. On September 4, 2016, Mother Teresa was canonized as Saint Teresa.

Come and take a bumpy ride with me into the mountains of transformation where you will discover the Black Madonna.

Something is waiting for us to make ground for it.

Something that lingers near us, something

that loves, something that waits

for the right ground to be made

so it can make its full presence known.

Dr. Clarissa Pinkola Estés

Chapter One

LA FAMILIA (THE FAMILY)

Ringlets bounced around my freckled ten-year-old face as I gathered firewood from the woodpile. I protected my hands from splinters by gently picking up each log. The Christmas scent of evergreen took me back to the San Juan Mountains, named after Saint John the Baptist, holy peaks where we had gathered *leña* (wood). When the *champes* (rosehip berries) turned orange, Grandpa Felipe drove his grandchildren in his '53 tan Chevy truck to La Jara Reservoir with all of us dangling from the sides of the pickup. Standing in the back of the truck, I felt free with my long curls flying in the air, the dust powdering my cheeks, and clean mountain air filling my lungs. Yellow and lavender columbines trumpeted in the lush green meadows full of aspen trees. The gulches in the road swallowed me, then tossed me high into the air where I could almost kiss the bluebird-colored sky. When Grandpa drove up to a fence, he slammed on his brakes. I jumped off the truck, then lifted and opened the chained gate. After Grandpa drove through, I encircled the heavy chain around the post and clasped the link over the nail. This was repeated at several locations until we had gathered enough wood to warm his house during Colorado's long sub-zero winter.

As a child I was intimate with the mountain's flowers, birds, and deer, and the hills loved me, too. Although, as my birthdays passed, my close connection with Nature got lost somewhere in the background. But a powerful archetype, which I came to know as the Black Madonna, was holding this important relationship with the natural world until later, when a pressure created an inner earthquake of major change within me.

Until then, I was a kid who had lots of chores, growing up in the '60s. Inside my house, the kindling box was almost filled, making this my last trip outside. With my arms layered with wood, I walked back to the kitchen. A rush of hot air radiating from the cast-iron stove greeted me. The lid on the pot of beans and chili rattled as spicy vapors escaped into the air. I saw Mom with flour dusted on her apron made of fabric with bright pink roses. She even had flour speckles on her hair, which was usually the color of ripened barley in August. Her hazel-colored eyes watched closely as I walked across the linoleum floor and dropped the kindling into the worn-out box next to the stove.

The kitchen was the heart of our family gatherings. An outsider, looking in, might see chaos. "Stop running in the house," Mom yelled to the little ones. On a typical Sunday morning after Mass, Mom crumbled red chili in the blender with garlic, salt, and water for *chili caribe*. Daddy made coffee, while Vivien fried potatoes and bacon and Veronica poured pancake batter on the hot griddle. In this commotion, our love for each other was marinating. I knew this was my home where I was fed and where I felt needed. Who else could set the table with a fork on a napkin placed to the left—or was it to the right?—of the dinner plate? Anyway, for sure my family had a fork and a napkin. On my birthday in January, a birthday cake and a special meal, maybe even a steak or baked chicken, was always planned.

Where else could I sit shoulder to shoulder around a large kitchen table with laughter filling the room as we played *canasta*, a card game that was passed down from my great-grandparents? This love-in-motion was my invisible security blanket that I carried with me. Even though my sisters and I fought with each other, God help the person who picked on one of us. I was their fierce protector.

Clap-clap-clap-clap.

Mom bounced the soft dough from one palm to the other until she threw it on the cast-iron skillet.

"Cindy, hot tortillas."

Mom only had to call me once. I could already taste the melted butter on the soft bread with crunchy bubbles. I was Mom's little helper, and she rewarded me by cooking my favorite foods with her loving hands.

My six sisters also loved Mom's cinnamon rolls, coconut cream pie, and *empanadas* (turnovers) filled with *queso* (homemade white cheese) and sprinkled with cinnamon. Vivien and Veronica (V&V) were active teenagers and rode motorcycles with their boyfriends. I often recruited my younger sisters to help gather eggs. Standing at the gate of the chicken coop were nine-year-old Janey and the three little ones: Viola, Ann, and Rosalie.

"Rosalie, here's the rock. Is it too big for you?"

"No." She opened her small hands, and I placed the big rock in her palms.

"Now, just like usual, go and drop it on the rooster's head. Okay?" She nodded her head.

The rest of us walked behind her as she released the rock on the rooster's head. Rosalie had dropped rocks on the rooster so many times that he was now afraid of her. He looked dazed and wobbly. The rest of us scattered like pollen in the wind, then quickly gathered the eggs and carefully placed them in the pail lined with straw. I snatched Rosalie, and we all ran out before the rooster could attack us.

Daddy was unable to help us, because at that time he worked construction hundreds of miles away in Denver. Eventually, he was able to find a job closer to home.

To maximize Mom's limited food budget, she planted peas, string beans, corn, and *calabacitas* (squash). In the fall, she bought crates of Palisade peaches that she canned in heavy syrup, and she froze green chili from New Mexico. She also gathered all her daughters like chicks and drove us to weekly Mass. I helped Mom by baking and often made cream puffs that overflowed with fresh cream from Bessie, our dear cow. When Rosalie needed a First Communion dress, I stayed up till midnight sewing the little dress for her sacramental day.

In the San Luis Valley, many times by Halloween, several feet of snow fell on the valley floor. Janey and I went trick-or-treating in La Jara, a town that had only five hundred people but with lots of chocolate candy. I was leading the way to the next house when I glanced over my shoulder and noticed Janey was whimpering. In puzzlement, I turned around.

"What's wrong, Janey?"

"The Ortiz brothers grabbed my bag of candy."

"Whhhat?" The Ortiz brothers were big boys, but I could care less about their size. I left Janey with the other trick-or-treaters and started walking around. Finally, I saw their figures through the dark night. I walked up to them; they were double my height and triple my weight.

"You give my little sister her candy back, right now!" Without saying a word, one of the boys, with the candy bag in his palm, pushed me into the air, and I landed on top of a snowbank. I slid down the ice and snow like I was riding a sled and landed on my butt on the sidewalk. I stood, shook the snow off my jacket and pants, and picked up the bag of candy they had left behind. I was a little shaken, surprised by my courage and surprised that it had worked, but I managed to walk back to Janey.

Gritting my teeth, I pushed the bag into Janey's hands. "Don't you ever let anyone steal your candy." We continued walking to the next house while eating our chocolate as if the Ortiz boys had never walked on the planet. Mom had appointed the right person to protect my little sisters.

We knew how to have fun, too. My little sisters, cousins, and I frolicked in the *acequia*, an irrigation system that has been traced to the Muslim Moors, who brought the system to Spain, and then the Spaniards used it in the land of Mexico. The murky water in the dirt-lined irrigation ditches brought relief from the hot summer afternoons. During the springtime, the snowpack high in the Continental Divide melted into the Alamosa River and from there was diverted to irrigation ditches established with water rights from the 1800s. The *acequia* was my Pacific Ocean. Like a dolphin, I dove into the three-foot chilly water and then sunbathed on the pebble embankment as if it were a white sandy beach in Maui.

Not only did I feel Nature's love, but I felt Daddy's love too, displayed by his generous hugs and kisses. When I told

Daddy about the Ortiz boys on Halloween night, he smiled with delight and pride. He said, "That's my girl." Daddy's name was Tiofilo, Greek for "lover of God." He was handsome and stood tall with his straw cowboy hat tipped to the side, partially covering his black wavy hair. He had the heart of a Native American Indian. When he plowed and planted his alfalfa, he was connected to the earth that he honored and loved.

I was amazed that Daddy had so much affection to give to others in spite of losing his mother Celina when he was only sixteen years old. Celina was pregnant with her fifteenth child when she hemorrhaged to death. The doctor had warned Celina not to get pregnant again. She had already had a miscarriage and had lost a daughter shortly after birth. Celina left behind nine daughters and four sons, ranging from sixteen months to twenty years old. For her wake, her children stood together like beads of a rosary encircling her casket that was placed in her bedroom. Her death overwhelmed many relatives.

Tia Rose had leaned against *Tio* Polito and cried, "How could God take a mother away from her children?"

Even though Grandma Celina had died prematurely at forty-five years of age, she planted a perennial seed of love in Daddy's heart that bloomed every day of his life. His capacity to love helped carry his brothers and sisters through their tremendous emotional loss.

La familia—the family's pulsating force—sustained me

as a young girl, too. This lifeblood was no different than the *acequia*, the ditches lined with dirt that irrigated this arid land with water. My heritage was rich in Spanish blood and my paternal great-grandmother was Navajo. My ancestors walked this land in southern Colorado that touched the New Mexico border, land that first was ruled by Spain, then Mexico, and finally the United States.

The farm and the family were connected by dirt roads shaded by cottonwood trees. Oftentimes, I skipped past the Chinese elms on my way to Grandpa Juanito's adobe house where he waited with candy or an invitation to the cookie jar. Grandpa lived 125 short steps from home. He was a county commissioner for twenty years and loved being involved in the community. I could not imagine someone like me, who was rowdy, going to long boring meetings. As a patriarch, Grandpa lived in his home until his death. He often said in Spanish, "If death comes knocking on my door, tell it I'm not home." Finally, he answered the door to death two weeks after his 100th birthday.

The red corrals and barns were 167 long steps from Grandpa's house, and they served as a gathering spot to meet up with our cousins, who lived a quarter mile away. All the action took place there, contrary to the pastoral scene of bulls and cows grazing in the meadow grass and seeking shade under the cottonwood trees. During irrigation season, a watering hole magically appeared in the high grass while birds flew from tree to tree squawking, "*Meee, meee,*" and some were whistling as if they were flirting with me!

To add some excitement to this serenity, I liked teasing Dino, the young black bull. Standing close to the four-foot barbwire fence, I tried to get his attention by waving my arms and shaking my hips. I shouted, "*Toro, toro!*" He turned his head, then lowered his maturing horns and charged me.

I ran and jumped over the barbed wire fence like a deer. Adrenaline shot through my trembling body. As soon as I landed on the other side of the fence, I looked to see how close Dino had gotten. He stood snorting several feet away. That was a close one!

In the background of the meadow stood Mount Blanca, 14,000 feet high. Oftentimes, it lived up to its name, capped with white snow that looked like frothy meringue. This was the crown of the Sangre de Cristo and the San Juan Mountain ranges. As an adult, I learned that Mount Blanca was known to the Navajos as Tsisnaasjini, or White Shell Mountain. Luci Tapahonso, Diné poet, wrote about this lofty mountain, "Blanca peak is adorned with whiteshell. Blanca peak is adorned with morning light . . . She is the brightness of spring. She is changing woman returned . . . Because of her we think and create."

The mountains inspired Grandma Rosana's quest to be an herbalist. Grandpa Felipe and Grandma Rosana, who were my godparents, lived several miles away, closer to the town of

Capulin—too far for me to walk or ride my bike. When Mom and I visited them, a minty whiff of *yerba buena* (spearmint) floated in the air of the kitchen. I found my seat at the bottom of the arch that separated the kitchen from the living room. It was a good place to sit and observe the happenings in Grandma's kitchen. Grandma was an herbalist who gathered her *remedios* (remedies) from the San Juan Mountains. She gathered *osha* (also known as Chuchupate or bear medicine) for skin and respiratory ailments, *chamiso heidondo* (sagebrush) to release body waste and toxins, and *poleo* and *yerba buena* for stomachaches.

Grandma and Mom were emotionally close, except they never agreed about these *remedios*. Sitting around the kitchen table that was near the wood-burning stove, Mom and Grandma separated pebbles from the pinto beans. I heard Grandma say, "Priscilla, herbs don't work for you, because you don't believe in them. You must have faith in them. Try *yerba buena*. It will help your stomach." Mom's stomach always ached, and she was prone to bleeding ulcers.

Without saying a word, Mom stayed focused on cleaning the beans. I only heard the pebbles rolling across the table. Grandma was right. Mom refused to drink Grandma's *remedios*, even if it meant she remained sick in bed.

At home, perhaps what was contributing to Mom's ulcers was having to take care of all her daughters, including two teenagers. To keep a constant eye on her socially active teens required much more time and effort than Mom had. So, starting when I was in fourth grade, for many years I was Mom's extra hand. Mom gave me the monumental task of being her eyes and ears with V&V, especially when they were around their boyfriends. Unfortunately, with this position came double trouble.

While Mom cooked macaroni and cheese, she turned to me, "What are Vivien and Veronica up to? You tell them they need to get in the house *right now*."

I jumped to attention like a soldier. I relished that our roles had switched. Now I could boss V&V around. I was tired of taking their orders:

"Cindy, clear the table."

"Wash the dishes."

"Get the jeans off the clothesline."

Now, with Mom's blessing I could push them around.

A distant humming increased to a loud noise as motor-cycles raced in and skidded to a stop in the backyard. The shiny metal on the maroon and turquoise bikes reflected the sun's rays. V&V sat on the idling machines and laughed with their boyfriends, who wore skin-tight black leather pants and worn leather jackets. By today's standards, my sisters were responsible adolescents, but they were charmed by a wild and rebellious flair and simply loved riding motorcycles with their boyfriends. I envied their excitement when they squeezed into their boyfriends for warmth or when the wind blew their hair.

Mimicking Mom's authority, even though I was only ten years old, I pushed the wood screen door open, tucked my hand into my waist, and flung my hip.

"Vivien and Veronica, Mom wants you in the house *right now*."

With that demand, their giggles, their long kisses, and their sizzling daydreams were cut short. They gritted their teeth as they slid off the motorcycles and finally let go of their boyfriends.

I was too young to realize that my sisters considered me a spy. A few months later, one night I rolled out of bed. My toes touched the cold linoleum floor as I walked toward the bathroom. Out of nowhere, Vivien grabbed my arm, and Veronica slammed me against the plaster kitchen wall. Vivien's curls were as tight as corkscrew spaghetti, and Veronica's freckles were as hot as bonfires. Veronica, forever Vivien's sidekick and known for her demure smile, rose to the occasion and held me down with brutal force.

Vivien held a splintered piece of firewood over my head. "If you tell Mom and Dad, we'll kill you."

I was confused about what I had done to make them so angry, but really, did it matter in this life-or-death situation?

As I looked up at the sharp splinters pointed at my eyes, in my child's mind, I felt I had only seconds to live. Suddenly, I realized that if I stopped snitching, they might let me go. I rolled my eyes downward in a submissive manner, which conveyed that I got their threat. They released their grip—for now. I had learned an important lesson: my observations only got me into trouble, even when I thought I was helping Mom. Without a doubt, I knew I would not be sharing this escapade with my parents. Not breathing a word was my only option. I tried to ignore V&V and their social plans. And from there on, my voice was silenced.

When Vivien graduated from high school and moved to Denver, Veronica and I remained at home. The triangle had been broken, and Veronica and I became closer. Decades later, loud motorcycles and fringed black leather jackets were only fond memories. Veronica yearned to get as far away from home as possible. Sometimes, Mom and Daddy had terrible fights. I would gather my little sisters in the back bedroom, so that they would be too far away to hear their angry words. Mom had locked the door to her heart without giving Daddy and her children the key. So Veronica was going to find this acceptance in God. She entered the convent, and, as a missionary nun, she found love in the heart of the Peruvians who lived high in the Andes. Vivien married and continued living in Denver.

When V&V left the farm, I was almost sixteen and ready to drive. Once I passed the driver's exam, I was free to drive wherever I wanted, and I drove fast. I loved the feeling of the car driving through the air. My version of riding a motorcycle. No one could stop me, except...

One day, I was driving down the lane when I saw Grandpa Juanito herding sheep to the corrals. For decades, raising sheep had been his bread and butter. Some of the old-timers remembered when white fuzzy fur could be seen as far as the horizon. On that day, I was too impatient, and the lambs were too slow, so I hit the car's horn. The lambs panicked and scattered in a hundred different directions. Grandpa ran to direct them toward the corrals. Looking at me with his anger that I had never seen before, he mumbled some Spanish words that I tried not to understand. In the future, I slowly drove through the herd of lambs while I recited: *Mary had a little lamb, the fleece was white as snow. And everywhere that Mary went the lamb was sure to go.*

My social life was going in its own direction as well. I was dating upperclassmen and watching movies with my girlfriends. I was thinking about my future and possibly attending college. I was interested in psychology as a result of Mom and some of my other relatives who grew up in alcoholic families. I saw their anger and their inability to build healthy relationships.

I remembered when one of Mom's favorite brothers passed away. She was crying, and I yearned to comfort her. I started to put my arms around Mom, but she pushed me away.

I was hurt, but I understood how hard it was for her to receive my tenderness. For a millisecond, I saw Mom as an abandoned child, perhaps a small reflection of myself. On the other hand, she displayed her love by cooking our favorite foods and taking good care of us.

I thought that perhaps, if people confronted their inner woundedness, like Mom's, they could enjoy the sweetness of love in their lives. Psychology or counseling might be the way to help them. In May, 1971, I graduated from high school and received a scholarship to Colorado State University in Fort Collins, Colorado. I was the first person in my immediate family to attend college, although I had many uncles and aunts who were college or professional school graduates. I was nervous about whether I could succeed at Fort Collins, especially living so far away from my family.

Chapter Two

ALMA MATER (CHERISHING OR FOSTERING MOTHER)

Many students who attended Colorado State University (CSU) were from rural areas in Colorado and other states. CSU was known for its veterinary, forestry, and agriculture departments. In high school, I had participated in a student council conference in Fort Collins; its farms and foothills reminded me of home. When I returned as a student, I was familiar with the student center and the dorms. I came to love CSU. It provided a newfound freedom, which lifted me as high as an eagle. No more worries about my little sisters or having to help Mom! Sewing a First Communion dress, baking chocolate chip cookies for Daddy, and cleaning the house were not my concerns anymore. All I had to do was take care of myself, which required more effort than taking care of others. I had to earn grades that fulfilled my scholarship requirements, which demanded I improve my studying habits. I can vividly remember the shock when I failed my first test. Skimming over notes the night before the exam was no longer going to achieve an "A."

It did not take long for my enthusiasm to wane, especially when I attended Sunday Mass at church a few blocks from campus. I watched families file into pews, and I wondered if their Mom was going to cook double-decker enchiladas for Sunday dinner or fried chicken with mashed potatoes and gravy.

Money was short and so were long distance telephone calls. Even though Mom and Dad were unable to financially support me, they cared about me in other ways. They wrote letters and sent bags of potatoes with me when I returned to school after the holidays. If I was lucky, I would also find a package of frozen T-bone steaks in the bag.

In my freshman year, my roommate, Lesley, introduced me to her best friend's boyfriend, Mark, who was a graduate of the Air Force Academy and was pursuing a master's degree in mathematics at CSU. Lesley's friend was attending college far away in California. Mark, his friend Gene, Lesley, and I often gathered for social activities. One night as we all were coming back from a movie, Mark was driving, and I was sitting in the back seat positioned in his rear view mirror. He stared into my eyes and said, "You have beautiful eyes."

Mark's Irish-blue eyes were equally as intriguing. I was uncertain whether he had Irish blood, but those eyes were the remnant of some Irish connection. He often used his fingers to comb his chestnut-colored hair. One day, Mark asked me out to a movie. During the movie, he slowly placed his arm around my shoulders. From then on, our group activities dwindled down to the two of us. Mark loved mathematics, and it was fun to watch someone who was so passionate about numbers—a subject that I struggled with. I had some competition when he was lying on the carpet in his apartment watching Star Trek, eating popcorn, and solving mathematical equations. But he made time for me. I nicknamed him Buddy, because we talked about everything, except one topic: the girlfriend in California. As we were getting more serious, Mark had to choose. I was afraid that I was going down the wrong path to romance and I would soon be walking off an emotional cliff. Mark's details were sketchy, but they broke up.

Mark grew up in the Pacific Northwest in a military family who had lived in exotic countries like Japan. He recounted trips to Europe while I only imagined what it was like. My world became bigger and more exciting traveling vicariously through his adventures.

Mark had lost his mother when he was twelve years old. She had died of lung cancer, and Mark detested when people smoked. His father chose to remain in the Air Force while his grandparents, who had English and Irish roots, raised him and his two little brothers. Eventually, Mark and his siblings joined his father and new wife. Maybe all that instability made him want to be settled with me.

Mark and I celebrated my birthday in Denver. I ate my first Oysters Rockefeller at a fancy restaurant there. I had only tasted canned oysters that Daddy often ate with saltine crackers. But there was no comparison to these oysters that were drenched in a buttery cream sauce topped with spinach. And other times, on frigid winter nights, we snuggled next to each other and walked to the local cafe for hot chocolate.

Mark's Ford Pinto took me to places where ordinarily it was too far for me to walk. Late one night, we drove to Horsetooth Reservoir above Fort Collins. We parked, and I rolled down the car's window. At a distance, perhaps at the other side of the reservoir, I heard dogs madly barking. Then all of a sudden an invisible presence held me down and gagged my mouth. No matter how much I tried to yell for Mark's help, not a sound, whimper, or scream could I make. Desperation turned me into a shivering prisoner. Mark turned on the ignition and started driving down the dirt road. When he drove around a curve, I was released from some invisible force. Mark and I looked at each other, and I almost started crying with fright.

"Did you feel that? I felt frozen."

With his eyes on the road, he said, "I felt like someone was controlling me, too."

Mark drove down the mountain as fast as he could. He

parked at my dorm, kissed me, and said, "I'll be calling you later."

I walked straight to my room. I ignored the TV room and my friends who were congregated in the hall. I used the bathroom, jumped into bed, snuggled into my pillow, and shook my head thinking, *What in the world was by Horsetooth?* We never found out what caused this paranormal experience, and we never returned to the reservoir again. Years later, I would be in a similar position trying to bring understanding to another inexplicable situation.

For Christmas break, Mark wanted to visit me at home. I had only been away for four months, and I did not think my parents would appreciate it if I brought home a boyfriend so soon. I told him "no." So, was I ever shocked that, on his own accord, I saw him driving his Ford Pinto down our dirt road. My parents liked him, but they were apprehensive about this new kid from the Northwest. My little sisters on the other hand were smiling hostesses as they offered, "Would you like some water or how about some cookies?"

As it turned out, we only had two quarters together at CSU, because he graduated and was reassigned to Williams Air Force Base in Arizona. I was hoping he would be reassigned somewhere in Colorado. We had spent so much time together that I knew my life would feel empty without him.

Before Mark left CSU, I wanted to be initiated as a

coed, making it official that I was a woman attending college. This initiation required that I be kissed at the Quad under a full moon at midnight. This ritual was part of the culture on campus. I asked Mark if he was interested.

"No, that's too late. I'll be sleeping."

"Okay, I really wanted you to make me a coed, but I'm sure I'll be able to find someone else."

Suddenly he changed his mind, and before I knew it, we were standing under a canopy of maple trees with the rays of the moon filtering through the branches. I stood on my tiptoes and made sure that wherever he was, he would remember this kiss. Four years later, two weeks after my graduation, we were married.

After our wedding in Colorado, we returned to Arizona where Mark worked at the pilot training center at Williams Air Force Base. Pilots came from all over the world to train there. For the next two years, he was busy working with the training simulators while I studied for a master's degree in counseling at Arizona State University.

Mark had bought a house in the desert with barren landscape around it. I tried to appreciate Arizona's climate, but walking on campus when it was 116 degrees was unbearable. On the other hand, I did appreciate the hot weather that produced citrus fruit in the winter and watermelons in the summer. The warm weather was conducive to the early morning jogging that kept us fit. Then we met Nat and Mary, first generation Italians, who had moved from New York to retire in Arizona. They taught us how to play bridge, which greatly enriched our social life. Their Italian values of the importance of family were a reminder of my Hispanic culture. They were my family away from home. Their friendship and playing bridge for hours helped me cope with the stress of graduate school.

Academically, my classes required hours upon hours of studying. Undergraduate studies seemed easy compared to this school. Some days I never stepped out of the house, because I had so much work to do. My studies emphasized cognitive and behavior therapies. My thesis was entitled *The Effects of Burnout in the Helping Profession.*

My program required that I complete personal psycho-therapy to become familiar with the psychotherapeutic process, as well as to examine the dynamics of my psyche. Being conscious of my own issues would bring clarity in the professional psychotherapeutic relationship. In our therapy relationship, I realized that trust was essential in establishing a rapport with my therapist. My lack of confidence in completing my studies emerged in our sessions. My fellow students were so competent and intelligent that I thought I had to work extra hard. But in time I established relationships with my professors, and I became more confident. And I always had Mary and Nat and our bridge games to help alleviate my stress level.

After two years, I received my master's degree in counseling. Mark completed his commitment to the military and decided to enter civilian life as a manager at The Boeing Company in Seattle, Washington. Before moving to Seattle, we splurged and traveled to Rome to attend midnight Mass. It was a Christmas Eve never to be forgotten! The newly elected Pope John Paul II was going to celebrate his first midnight Mass at the Papal Basilica of Saint Peter. Only about ten feet from the aisle, Mark squeezed my hand and grinned as we watched John Paul, radiating with holiness and humility, walking in the processional. He was medium height, barrel chested, and fit as an athlete who was ready to run around the world to bring justice to the human soul. The future saint's motto was *Totus Tuus* (Totally Yours, Mary). After this memorable Roman holiday, we continued our adventures to London, Athens, and different cities in Germany.

Moving to the Pacific Northwest from the Arizona desert in January, 1979, did not make for the easiest transition. The drizzling rain never stopped. I fell asleep and woke up to the continuous tap-tap of the rain. When the sun finally broke through the clouds, one radio commentator referred to it as a UFO.

After a couple of years, Mark and I started discussing having children. We had been married for four years. Having children was a big decision for me. I was jumping in with my eyes wide open, with no idealistic notions about raising children. Mom had worked hard and sacrificed a lot. Instead of buying herself a new Easter dress, she used the money to buy each of us a Sunday dress with a matching hat and purse.

The biggest roadblock to having children was my terror about childbirth. As an adolescent I had suffered from severe menstrual cramps. Today, it would be diagnosed as endometriosis, a gynecological condition that affects millions of women. Sometimes, when the pain was unbearable, Mom drove me to the hospital emergency room. The doctor ordered a pain shot that put me to sleep for the rest of the day.

Mom tried to help me by scheduling an appointment with our family doctor.

After the doctor examined me, he looked at me and said, "Once you have babies, you'll be fine."

I wanted to grab the stethoscope hanging around his neck and yell, "I'm only fourteen years old, and babies couldn't be further from my mind. I desperately need your help now!" I believed that the doctor's religious beliefs regarding having as many children as possible compromised my medical care.

Instead, Mom and I walked out of the room without a treatment plan, and I had to face years of unbearable pain. Mom trusted the doctor, and I was too immature to question him. Finally, in college I visited the campus doctor, and he prescribed birth control medication that completely eliminated my pain. I could have kissed him. I had finally found a doctor who listened to my concerns.

Unfortunately, during my teenage years of excruciating pain, Vivien had advised me, "Menstrual pain is nothing compared to childbirth."

"I'll never be able to have a child," I mumbled.

At age twenty-seven, I was right smack in the face of my biggest fear. I was searching for someone who would sympathize with me. I knew Mom had no idea what I would be going through, because for some medical reason she did not feel labor pain when she delivered her seven daughters. Years ago during my adolescence, she had helped all she could by taking me to the doctor.

Out of nowhere, the Virgin Mary popped into my mind. Certainly, she was afraid of delivering her baby, no matter how many divine signs came to her. She must have felt isolated from her community, given her unusual circumstances with Joseph. So, I started praying to her when I found out that I was pregnant, hoping that she would give me the courage to endure labor pains. With the Virgin Mary's friendship, I did not feel alone anymore, and—like millions of other women—I would get through childbirth, too. Marissa was born in 1980, and, twenty-six months later, Andrea was our special gift. Vivien was wrong. Childbirth was not as severe as my menstrual cramps.

Unexpectedly, I became a total believer in *remedios*. Two

weeks before Andrea was born I had been diagnosed with Bell's Palsy, a facial paralysis. Ninety percent of my facial nerve on the right side of my face had died, possibly due to a virus, although each neurologist had his or her own theory. All I cared about was my facial disfiguration. The right side of my face drooped so badly that oftentimes my mouth drooled, and I needed a straw to sip water. I found it hard to blink my right eye. My neurologist prescribed an anti-inflammatory medication, and I used electric stimulation on my face.

Mom told Grandma about my Bell's Palsy. Grandma mailed a rose salve with the instructions via Mom, "Tell Cindy to rub the salve on her face several times a day." When I smoothed the salve over my drooped face, I felt like Grandma was rubbing her love into my skin while I smelled sweet rose petals. How could I feel isolated in this garden of roses? I had avoided people, because I refused to see their stares of shock. However, in my humiliation, I learned the importance of compassion towards myself and tenderness towards others who have residual effects from strokes, amputations, or other impairments. Grandma's rose salve did not regenerate my facial nerve, but she helped me to heal emotionally. She taught me how to be compassionate with others as she was with me.

I had just started my psychotherapeutic practice when Mark got caught up in the computer frenzy in Seattle. He and two other colleagues were itching to start a computer graphics company. One day he walked into the kitchen and said, "I think we found office space in a building close to Bellevue."

I continued chopping the salad. "Are you sure this is what you want?"

"Oh, we're sure."

There were so many risks in the computer business that it took a leap of faith to support Mark in this entrepreneurial venture. I was afraid of how the company might change our lives. I wanted to say, "Mark, sit down. We need to discuss some tough questions. We need to stop and think about how much of our personal and financial security will be sacrificed for this company, and will the sacrifice be worth it? What if we fail? I'm terrified, how about you?"

But my feelings and concerns refused to roll off my tongue, because often I minimized their value. It was easier to continue the role of the obedient daughter as the obedient wife who forfeited my insights to Mark's intelligence. In time, I became philosophical and convinced myself that this opportunity was no different than other choices we had made, especially moving to Seattle. I was comforted by thinking that in life there were no guarantees, just fertile ground for personal growth. Age was on our side. Mark was thirty-four, and I was thirty-one. We believed in the world of possibilities where enthusiasm and hard work produced success. Nothing in my awareness could have prepared me for the unbelievable stress that lay ahead.

The three founders started a computer graphics company. Mark, as CEO, worked sixteen-hour days and traveled to all parts of the country securing necessary business contracts. Mark and I hosted business dinners and parties. I strove to be admired by Mark and our guests as a gracious hostess and a gourmet cook.

Not only did the company's social life keep me busy, but our daughters kept me hopping with driving them to Montessori School or to ballet, baton, and swimming lessons. As four-year-old Marissa threw her baton in the air, with her pale complexion and long eyelashes sweeping over her dark espresso eyes, I could not help but think of Disney's Snow White. When two-year-old Andrea jumped out of the pool drenched in water, her pixie haircut framed her doe-like eyes and smiley face. In a fundraiser for the American Heart Association, she raised hundreds of dollars by swimming the most lengths of the pool. Like all proud parents, I adored my little girls.

And to top it off, my private practice was growing. As a psychotherapist, I had appointments with adults and couples in the afternoon and evenings. I belonged to a group of psychotherapists who met every week for peer consultation. This peer review was helpful in evaluating my clients and elevating my skill level. I loved working with my clients, but it was difficult squeezing my work into our busy schedule.

Marissa and Andrea often heard this dialogue as I tried

to get Mark's attention while he gathered his papers in his briefcase:

"I need to leave for work by early afternoon. Can you pick up the girls at the babysitter?"

"I'll try, but I'm preparing a brief. Remember, I'm leaving tomorrow. I'll be gone until the end of the week."

"Okay, I might have some cancellations. I'll call you." At the time, neither of us noticed that more often than not, I adjusted my schedule to meet his needs.

I strove to be a super mother, wife, and psychotherapist and to accomplish the most in the shortest amount of time, even if it caused stress and, at times, excruciating colitis. But I refused to spend the time figuring out what was triggering this painful condition. Taking medication was the fastest solution.

If I had started digging too deep, I might have realized that I was becoming a single parent with too much responsibility and not enough down time for myself. Mark was simply not around when he worked fourteen- or sixteen-hour days and traveled the rest of the time. Oftentimes, he came home exhausted and walked straight to bed.

One Easter weekend I was making holiday plans. "Mark, how about if we either go out for dinner, or I can make dinner here. But it might be more special to eat at a nice restaurant."

"You know I need to rest. Why don't you take the girls out, and I'll sleep?"

"Okay." My eyes started blinking with tears.

Even if I had wanted to talk or argue with Mark, I had convinced myself that these were the sacrifices I needed to make in order for us to build a successful business. I felt that Mark was so preoccupied with the company that he was incapable of listening to me. In truth, I was unwilling to listen to myself and open the door to my resentments. If I had, I would have felt my anger, which stemmed from being alone so much. I was hesitant about starting this company, because I was afraid that our life would deteriorate, and it did. Yet I packed away my feelings as if I could store them away in boxes. I was unwilling to have Marissa and Andrea grow up with parents who were always fighting like my own parents did. At the time, I did not realize that my parents' fighting helped them reach their forty-eighth wedding anniversary.

Two years had passed since Mark cofounded the company when one day, as I was picking up toys in the family room, I felt a tugging of some kind. It was as if someone were tapping my shoulder. I stood up and turned around. No one was there. Actually, I was the only one in the house. I had never before experienced this mysterious sensation. It continued for months, and I ignored it for months. But the pulling was as real as Andrea grabbing my skirt for attention. But with this sensation, I could not see or hear a soul.

Finally, I asked myself, what is trying to get my attention? Unlike my colitis pain, this tugging was not emanating within my physical body. It was coming from a place outside of myself. It was such an annoyance that, as a psychotherapist, I knew that I had to stop and reflect on how my life was continually changing and evolving. Someone looking in might have said, "Are you sure these are the changes you want?"

I searched for answers by attending a Lenten series within my Roman Catholic faith, and I participated in workshops in the fields of psychology and self-development. I thought that the answer lay there. Unfortunately, neither shed light on the strange tugging sensation.

I continued reflecting on my life. Was the source of this tugging the cultural void of missing my Hispanic heritage and my home in Colorado's San Luis Valley that I yearned for? Seattle's scenery was like gazing into an emerald stone, beautifully lush in the summer and hard and cold during the bone-chilling winter. What I would give to feel the hearth warmth of Mom's kitchen stove as she was cooking tortillas. I could taste the homemade *capulin* (chokecherry) jam that I smeared on the bread. It was as if Mom kneaded her motherly affection into the wet flour, then rolled her love into circles to feed my heart and soul. In Colorado, I had so many relatives who, if I had asked, would have helped me with Marissa and Andrea. And there would have been so many dinners and parties that we could have partaken in. Sometimes, as I was sitting in my dining room in Seattle, I imagined my sisters and parents gathered around our big dining room table eating crab and oysters with their laughter filling our sometimes lonely house.

The questions continued: Was there something missing in my life? Was I living to my fullest potential? Was I fulfilling my life's purpose? What more was I supposed to accomplish? My outer life with a beautiful home, two precious daughters, a growing practice, and a husband thriving in the computer industry satisfied all my needs. What more could I possibly need or want? What more was needed to complete my life?

But something had its grip on me, and it was not letting go. If I could have given it words, it would have said, "I demand that you recognize me." But who was "me"? As a psychotherapist, I had guided others to listen to their forgotten parts and reclaim their voices, whether it was emotionally or spiritually. Had I missed a critical piece in my own life?

Several months later, my colleague Joan announced a seminar in Switzerland on Process-oriented Psychology founded by Arnold Mindell, a Jungian analyst. Relationship work, mythology, theory and process structures, dreamwork, bodywork, collective processes, and comparative medical concepts were listed as the curriculum. At first, I was the observer, listening to my colleagues' enthusiastic plans to attend this seminar. Then it somehow changed into my plan: dreamwork and relationship work sounded interesting. What am I going to pack for the trip? Is my passport still valid? Catching myself, I said, "Hold it!" How can I possibly be thinking about leaving my young daughters and my husband, who was traveling more than he was at home? Do I really think that I can leave my family for six weeks? My struggle between being the traditional mother, like my mother who loved to bake cookies and cakes from scratch, and being the professional psychotherapist who strove for growth volleyed back and forth in my mind: On one hand, like my own mother, I believed that a good mother does not leave her children for any reason. A good mother sacrificed everything for her family.

On the other hand, a master's degree in counseling and years of clinical experience were not enough in my profession. Continued education in different psychological modalities and personal growth were necessary in order to be an effective psychotherapist. At the time, I was unaware that this trip was connected to my inner tugging.

The conflict landed in Mark's court. While Mark and I discussed the possibility of the trip to Zürich, finally he realized that the only way I could attend this seminar was with his help. But I knew that was impossible. So he shocked me when he offered, "I'll limit my out-of-town meetings. I can be here for the girls in the evenings and nights, so you can go to Zürich."

I was taken aback, but at the same time, I grabbed his offer. "Yes! That makes all the difference in the world." All I needed was after-school care for Marissa and Andrea. Suddenly, I remembered a conversation with Pat, a neighbor who was looking for work. I telephoned her, and she agreed to the nanny position while Mark was at work.

The months of preparation flew by. Before I knew it, the trip was upon me. When it was time to drive to the airport, Mark, Marissa, and Andrea gathered in the foyer. But Marissa refused to go with us.

She slipped her thumb into her mouth and walked to the playroom. "Just take me to the babysitter."

I had learned that oftentimes children show their emotions through their behavior, whether through temper tantrums or sulking. Marissa was angry and was feeling that I was abandoning her. I grabbed Andrea's hand, and we walked into the playroom. I knelt beside Marissa, held her small body in my arms, and whispered, "I love you, sweetie." Then I looked at Andrea, and I realized that leaving my children was not an option. Within seconds, I reevaluated whether this seminar was such a great idea when it required me to travel thousands of miles away from my family. *Was I asking my family to sacrifice too much? Would Mark's company financially suffer because he would be unavailable to travel? How much money would I lose if I canceled the trip?* I almost convinced myself to call off the flight, but from some unknown place I got a burst of reassurance. It was as if a voice said, "Responsibility lies in the hands of others." This time it was not necessary to worry about taking care of my little sisters, my children, or my husband. It was healthy for me to lean on others.

When we drove Marissa to the babysitter's, she jumped out of the car holding closely her She-Ra Princess of Power doll without saying good-bye. Mark and Andrea drove me to the airport. Mark hummed one of his favorite Patsy Cline songs, "Crazy Love," while Andrea looked out the window. At the airport, we walked to the gate together. I turned and held Andrea and kissed her. "I promise to write you a letter every day, and I'll call once a week."

Then I turned to Mark and hugged him. "I love you."

To calm the butterflies in my stomach and the sadness in my heart on the flights to New York, Paris, and finally Zürich, I repeated the mantra, "I know I can take care of myself, and I know Mark can take care of himself and the girls."

Nothing in my awareness could have prepared me for the life-changing experience that was soon to spring forth in Switzerland. Little did I know that I would be more worried about me than my family in Seattle.

Chapter Three

THE MYSTERIOUS FEMININE

Hotel Zürich, a two-story bed and breakfast, was decorated with impeccable flower gardens that the Swiss, with their love for detail, meticulously manicured. Rose bushes—with their dramatic flair of royal purple and passionate red—enticed their admirers into a pool of emotions. No wonder gardening consumed the serious Swiss. After two weeks of intense classes and supervision, this weekend promised to bring much needed relaxation. However, before I could breathe a sigh of relief, there were rumblings of an international disaster. I could never have imagined that the dates Saturday, April 26, and Sunday, April 27, 1986, would change my life forever.

On Saturday, a Russian word pierced my consciousness: Chernobyl. In Pripyat, Russian children squealed and laughed as they imagined riding the Ferris wheel in the new amusement park that was to open on May Day. Instead, a reactor that was close to Pripyat exploded, and the fire sent a plume of highly radioactive dust over western Soviet Union,

Europe—Switzerland included—and eastern North America. Within thirty-six hours after the explosion, more than 49,000 people scrambled to pack their identity papers, food, and clothing. Years later, a piercing silence filled the air as deteriorated metal stood as a terrifying memorial to this environmental disaster.

That day, I was ready to catch the next flight back to Seattle. My first inclination was to go where I felt safe. A colleague tried to reassure me, "Don't worry; we'll be fine." The nonchalance of everyone—my colleagues, the instructors, and the hotel staff—irritated me. The Swiss were hardly known for their animated display of emotions, so I questioned whether I could trust their perceptions when they were so indifferent. I silently screamed at them, "You might not be worried or afraid, but I'm scared to death to be so far from my family. I don't want to die in Europe!"

This disaster was not part of my plan. All I could do was stay busy and avoid thinking about the possible consequences of this radioactive catastrophe. Somehow, not knowing the consequences was worse than knowing them.

The next day was Sunday, April 27. Joan, with whom I had shared clinical supervision for the last four years, was now my roommate. Joan was a seasoned therapist with over twenty-five years of clinical experience and from whom I had learned a lot. She strode into our room on her long legs. She asked: "Do you want to go with us to Einsiedeln (pronounced in German: "'ainzi:dln'") to visit the shrine of the Black Madonna?"

"Whose shrine?"

"The Black Madonna. Haven't you read about her?"

"No, not really." A more honest response would have been, "I absolutely have no idea what you are talking about." I minimized my ignorance about this Black Madonna and her chapel in Einsiedeln. I had no knowledge of the fact that it was one of Switzerland's greatest spiritual centers. All I was aware of was my fear of the Chernobyl catastrophe and not wanting to be left alone in Zürich.

My friends and I walked several blocks to catch the tram that would leave us at the Hauptbahnhof, one of the busiest train stations in the world. Our train was scheduled for 11:03 a.m., and the Swiss did not mean 11:02 or 11:04, but exactly 11:03. The Swiss dependability provided security when I was so unsure about the consequences of the Chernobyl disaster. Traveling to Einsiedeln occupied my mind, and I was confident that the church in Einsiedeln would provide the peace and calm that I desperately needed. When we hopped on the train, I settled in my seat with a bottle of water and, of course, my Swiss chocolate candy for the hour ride.

Through the train window, I noticed the rugged snow-covered peaks of the mighty Swiss Alps, the largest mountain range in Europe. Their foreboding steepness made me imagine a lion's white teeth ready to devour me. Thankfully, the mood changed as we scooted through Alpine villages with white steeple churches, providing idyllic peaceful scenery. Light brown cows roamed freely in the green velvet meadows as they slowly chewed the grass. I admired—well, okay—I loved these cows. They produced cream used for the most delectable chocolate I had ever tasted, a silky indulgence that piqued my senses and sent a tickle to the tips of my toes. I had read an article on *Schokolade* that stated, in the 1700s, the Zürich Council banned chocolate because it was unfit for virtuous citizens. My theory was that maybe the chocolate's aphrodisiac qualities were exactly what the Swiss needed to become more passionate. Oh yes, the Swiss have reached the pinnacle of perfection with their confection.

Between the smooth chocolate melting in my mouth and the train's rhythmic motion, my worries subsided. The train rocked me back and forth until I almost forgot that the purpose of the trip was to visit the shrine of the Black Madonna.

I was reminded of the trip's purpose when the train shrieked and jerked to a stop. I contorted my body to read the city sign "Einsiedeln" hanging above the platform. Single file, my friends and I followed each other off the train to a narrow cobblestone street shadowed by quaint gift shops. Oddly, each window was painted with two black ravens in flight. These birds must have held a special significance for this town, because their images were everywhere. A narrow slice of blue sky was immediately above me. The tunnel-like street was jammed with tourists. I was concentrating on my footing on the uneven cobblestone walkway, which made me oblivious to what was ahead.

Suddenly, when I stepped into a large plaza, a world of unbelievable grandeur awaited me. At a distance, a Benedictine Abbey, a Baroque sandstone structure the size of four city blocks, was in front of a thick Alpine forest as if the woods had given birth to this holy place. Around the semicircular plaza, the church and abbey looked like arms reaching out to hold me. Twin towers loomed high into the cloudless sky as their bells tolled, summoning pilgrims to the church. . . to the home of the Black Madonna.

On the periphery of the church, vendors sold rosaries, prayer cards, crosses, and books on the history of the Black Madonna of Einsiedeln. Nearby stood a statue of the Immaculate Conception crowned with a golden halo sprinkled with stars. Mothers and fathers sat relaxing on the church steps while their children jumped up and down the stairs, taking turns drinking water from a fountain fed by a spring. Contented families talked with each other as if this were their usual Sunday ritual: a time to be together and a place to be with their God. Their clothes were simple compared to the flashy gold watches and silk suits in Zürich. The pilgrims' weathered faces matched their weathered clothes, which reminded me of the farmers in southern Colorado where I grew up. There, too, we lived a life of simplicity grounded in our Catholic faith and our relationship with the land that gave us food, strength, and meaning.

On this unusually warm spring day, my hands cupped the fluid from the fountain, and I eagerly drank the cool water. As the water dripped from my lips, I gazed at the mammoth church and reflected: it seemed impossible that I was standing in front of such an ancient church in Switzerland thousands of miles away from home where I was racing from one place to the other.

Slate gray stairs stretched up to the church's entrance like a welcome mat. As I climbed, I felt as though each step was elevating me to a higher realm of consciousness where new ideas and different perspectives awaited me. Opening the heavy wooden door, I found a dark and refreshingly cool interior. The flair of the seventeenth century Baroque architecture evoked an experience of walking into a celestial garden. I looked up and saw a gleaming white ceiling painted with elaborate peach and pink roses wrapped in gold ribbon. Plaster angels with chubby cheeks poked out of the ceiling and looked like babies being born, not unlike myself in this time of grasping and searching. Much to my surprise, there was a large black marble shrine encasing an altar and a statue at the entrance of the church. Unlike most Catholic churches, where the only altar can be found in the sanctuary. This sacred place greeted me and the other pilgrims who entered.

Gathered around the shrine I heard pilgrims calling to the Madonna in different languages:

Santa Maria.

Vierge Marie.

Mutter Maria hilf mir.

Nostra Signora.

Not wanting to miss any excitement, I walked toward the shrine where a white marble altar was in front of a wooden statue. The shrine was encased in a wrought iron cage with a locked gate. Above the altar, I saw the statue of the Black Madonna—who was as black as a night sky—holding Baby Jesus on her lap, and Jesus was black, too. I was taken aback by their darkness. I was accustomed to Mary with a caramel-colored face like Our Lady of Guadalupe or with a pink complexion like Our Lady of Fatima, not this blackness. The Madonna was dressed in a beautiful red robe embroidered in gold. I knew from my Catholic upbringing that this was referred to as a "hanging."

I noticed wooden crutches that children, men, and women had discarded and had left hanging on the wall. These remnants were left behind as personal testimonies of their miracles with this Black Madonna. Hundreds of votive candles twinkled on each side of the massive wooden doors and left a scent of smoky melted wax.

I looked for a pew and knelt when a pilgrim caught my attention. Her hair was covered with a scarf, and she wore a white blouse tucked in a long cotton skirt. The Madonna mesmerized her. With a strong desire to emulate her deep devotion, I bowed my head, closed my eyes, and clasped my fingers together. Falling into this unknown world, I surrendered to the Madonna.

My curiosity and eagerness to know this mysterious woman coalesced into a spontaneous question: "What do you want me to hear?"

The Madonna's voice resonated within me, and she said with perfect clarity, "I'm going to take Marissa."

I was jolted out of this serene place that I had entered and gasped. Not my Marissa! I struggled, not wanting to acknowledge what I had heard. My body trembled. Did she mean that my daughter was going to die? How could she take my precious child away from me? If so, who was this black Virgin Mary, anyway?

To gain some control over the situation, I rebelled. No! I did not hear a thing within me. It was just my imagination. My mind denied her words, but my body refused to cooperate. I felt weak, and beads of perspiration bounced off my skin. The air seemed to be sucked out of the church and out of me. I managed to slide off the kneeler onto the pew. I needed fresh air, and I needed it now.

I stood and walked through the crowds until I reached the front door that I had walked through minutes earlier. Pushing the door open, the fresh air cooled my skin. I inhaled a full breath, as if my life depended on it, and continued to breathe and absorb the warm sunshine on my face. Leaving my colleagues behind without an explanation, I was determined to catch the next train to Zürich and *never* return to this church.

On the train back to Zürich, I hardly noticed the countryside. Nothing mattered. In a state of shock, I was unable to absorb the Madonna's words. When the *billeteur* asked for my ticket, I handed it to him, avoiding his eyes. I did not want to make contact with him or anyone else. When I arrived at the hotel I slipped into my room. I told no one of the words I heard from the Black Madonna, as if not talking about her would erase my experience. That night I wrestled with the Madonna's threatening words, and, when I woke up the next morning, my pillow was drenched with tears.

Still haunted by the Madonna's voice, I left for classes. Part of the training included studying process theory, practicing therapeutic skills, and working on my own personal issues. In my supervisory group, I requested to work as a client and asked another student to be my therapist. I sat in the center of the room facing my partner; my colleagues and other students sat in a circle around us.

I began. "Yesterday I traveled to Einsiedeln to visit the

shrine of the Black Madonna. In prayer when I asked the Madonna, 'What do you want me to hear?' she said, 'I'm going to take Marissa.'"

As I said these words, I felt a sharp pain between my eyebrows, as if someone had used their knuckles to punch my forehead. The pain left me breathless. In my confusion, I held my aching head. What was this pain about? The pain then disappeared as fast as it appeared. Sensing my distress, Dr. Josef, the supervisory therapist, intervened. "Let's stop the work. Cindy needs to continue in a private session."

My friends held me in their arms and tried to comfort me. "You're going to be okay." With their support, I was able to continue attending classes. That night I scheduled a private therapy session with Dr. Josef.

After dinner, I telephoned Mark in Seattle. I desperately needed to hear that Marissa was fine and that she was not in the hospital. Without alarming Mark, I gently explained what the Madonna told me. "How's Marissa doing? Is she sick?"

"She's fine."

"Does she ask for me?"

"No, not much. It's Andrea. She says, 'When's Mommy coming home?' I tell her it's going to be a few weeks. The girls love the postcards. They like the coffee-colored cows and the snowy mountains and the Swiss children."

"I told them I would write to them every day, and I meant it."

Mark continued detailing his work and his time with Marissa and Andrea. My mind wandered back to Seattle and my departure for Zürich. It was so uncharacteristic of Marissa to refuse to say good-bye. Maybe her behavior had been an omen, although Mark did not seem concerned about the Black Madonna's words.

"I love you, and tell Marissa and Andrea I love them, too. I miss them lots. Before you know it, I'll be home." Tears welled in my eyes. I did not want Mark to hear my sadness.

"I love you, too. And don't worry about the girls. They're doing fine."

After our conversation, I returned to my room. I was relieved that Marissa was doing well, but the uncertainty of Marissa's future was like a pestering bee. I was exhausted by several sleepless nights and by my emotional fatigue, which finally overcame me. At last, I was able to rest.

Four days later, I met with Dr. Josef in his counseling room. Dr. Josef had Einstein-like hair and looked like he had just stepped out of a science laboratory. He was a professor and a seasoned psychotherapist, so I was confident that he would provide the clinical structure and safety net to proceed with the session. I looked out a large square picture window that was in front of me, while I started recalling my encounter with the

Black Madonna. I saw aspen trees with shiny teardrop leaves that sparkled in the sunlight as they swayed in the gentle breeze. I watched the spring-green leaves in their hypnotic dance until my eyelids felt heavy and the pace of my words got slower. I felt like I was in a half-conscious state. Dr. Josef recognized this and said, "Follow this inner calling."

I completely closed my eyes and went into a dream-like place. I found myself sitting on a knoll of grass with a plethora of white daises with bright yellow faces gathered around me. I stood and walked through the meadow when I noticed a grove of trees with their branches shading a white altar. A woman, dressed in a dark brown cloak with a hood covering her head, waited for me. I was drawn to her and walked toward her. As I approached her, she opened her arms and took me into herself. The hood hid her face, but I knew she was the Black Madonna.

As I pressed against her body, I felt long, sagging breasts that reminded me of a grandmother who carried wisdom older than the sun and who was wiser than the seasons. Her body of boundless energy baptized me in an ocean of love and compassion. This rapture melted all boundaries as her love was within me and around me. Nothing existed except the totality of oneness with this infinite source of love. Like drops of dew in the sun, my questions about life, my insecurities, all my frailties, my disappointments, my anxiety about the Chernobyl disaster, and the uncertainty of Marissa's future instantly evaporated. Nothing existed but this infinite source of love, a refuge of bountiful motherly tenderness. I never wanted to leave her embrace.

I started to sense Dr. Josef's presence in the room, and the more I sensed his presence, the less I felt the Black Madonna's embrace. It felt as if a magnet were drawing me away from her, and I knew there was nothing I could do to stop it.

When I opened my eyes, I was in that twilight place between being asleep and being awake. I began to notice the white walls that surrounded me in the counseling room. Dr. Josef sat in front of me. I was no longer with the Black Madonna. Suddenly, a wave of loneliness flooded over me. The room that was once warm and comfortable now felt like a freezer, and I shivered in its cold. The old grandmother's blazing love seemed a universe away. Compared to being embraced in her compassion, I felt empty. I burst into tears.

I wiped away my tears but noticed that Dr. Josef was deep in thought. After I composed myself, he listened as I recounted my vision with the Black Madonna, who was as real as Dr. Josef sitting in front of me. He hesitated to interpret or analyze my encounter with the numinous Feminine.

As a psychotherapist, I knew that over-rationalizing would diminish the impact of this spiritual encounter. I needed time to absorb the Madonna's love and compassion and remain present in it. Logic would keep me in my head and out of my emotions and ultimately would negate the experience.

My understanding of the Black Madonna would come later. So with few words, Dr. Josef allowed the time and space for the experience to reveal its meaning. Before I knew it, the session was over.

I grounded myself into the here and now by curling my fingers and shaking my body. I reminded myself that no matter what spiritual heights I reached, I would always need to be fully present in my human body.

Later in the day, I noticed an extraordinary sensation: a current of energy streaming through me. It felt like a ball of static electricity traveling up and down my spine, localizing in my genital area above my pubic bone; it was a sexual/electric intensity that could have lit up New York City. I felt powerless to deal with this force. It was as if I had been literally embraced by the Madonna's power of love and compassion—a vital force that seeped into the cells of my body. Thankfully, in the evening the intensity subsided.

Weeks passed and final exams were my only obstacle to seeing Marissa and Andrea again. During an oral exam in medical concepts, the instructor asked, "What physical condition should be considered with the symptoms of difficulty in expressing emotions along with shortness of breath and tightness in the chest?"

"Asthma," I blurted.

My colleagues turned and stared at me. I just shrugged

my shoulders, since I genuinely did not know the source of the answer—not consciously, anyway. My response sprang from inside me. The professor asked another question, and again my answer bounced from some unfamiliar place. A colleague turned and said, "Good job."

Before a wave of academic superiority could wash over me, I recognized that something was different within me. I could not put my finger on it. These answers were not coming from my rational mind, but from a different source. But I was too excited about leaving for home to figure out the origin of this knowledge. After I said good-bye to my newfound friends, I left on the shuttle to the airport.

When I was boarding the plane, I saw a businessman who caught my attention and who wore a blue suit with a tie, similar to Mark's. When I relaxed in my seat, I suddenly realized that this tie and suit represented the corporate world, which was a noose strangling the life out of our marriage. Our relationship lacked any work/life balance. We did not have any time for intimate conversations or time to explore our emotional world. The stress that came from owning a company that now employed over a hundred people was the basis of our marriage.

I had tried to minimize the stress in our daily lives as best as I could. I kept the house organized and cleaned. I had even organized my inner house of feelings where my frustration was packed away in boxes, my loneliness was tucked away in a book, and my needs were hidden under the pillow. Our relationship had become rigid, with little spontaneity. One time, I wanted to go sailing. "Mark, I've always wanted to sail. We can rent a sailboat with a captain and travel around the San Juan Islands. Doesn't that sound exciting?"

"No, I have too much work to do."

I was so disappointed. I lacked the insight and guts to push the pause button and say, "Forget about your work for one weekend. We can schedule the sailing when it's most convenient for you. We can either take Marissa and Andrea with us, or we can get a babysitter for them." More importantly I needed to say, "The success of our marriage depends on our spending time together to reevaluate our lives and ask important questions like: 'How can we make each other feel as important as the company? How can we make each other happier? How can our love be the number one priority in this crazy life of ours?'"

Instead, I reverted back to a familiar place where I unknowingly placed a strip of tape across my mouth while I watched our marriage unravel.

During the flight to Seattle, the nine-hour trip gave me ample time to reflect. I asked the Black Madonna again, "What do you want me to hear?" and I finally recognized the issues in our marriage that I had ignored for several years. I had refused to realize that the man who had been my best friend and whom I had nicknamed Buddy had become a stranger. Earlier in our relationship, nothing in this world was more important than talking and sharing our feelings. Once the company was founded, there was a shortage of time, especially to share my deepest struggles about parenting. Sometimes I felt like a single parent, alone and yearning for closeness and reassurance that our marital struggles were only temporary.

I found this closeness I was looking for in the Madonna's divine love, yet it generated so many questions. Would I ever understand the meaning of the words, "I'm going to take Marissa"? I trembled with fear about the possibility of Marissa's bleak future. To reassure myself, I recognized that many people have spiritual experiences. I believed that mine was site-specific. The Madonna would remain in Einsiedeln, and I would continue my life in Seattle.

I was dead wrong.

Chapter Four

MEDITATION AS A REVOLVING DOOR
TO THE BLACK MADONNA

Mark, Marissa, and Andrea were waiting for me when I landed at Sea-Tac Airport. My welcome home bouquet was Marissa and Andrea's beautiful faces. I was hugging them and kissing their soft peachy cheeks. I was swept away with the safety and normalcy of being home. And I was happy to see Mark, too. "I am so grateful," I whispered in his ear with a kiss, "that you made my trip to Zürich a reality." I tucked away the revelations that had emerged about our marriage.

As I looked out the car window at the Emerald City, I noticed how the rains had carpeted the hills with velvety lushness. Everywhere I turned, I saw strokes of yellow daffodils and pink and white tulips. Even the pitter-patter of the rain sliding down the car's windows was melodic.

This verdant environment reminded me of the readings of Hildegard van Bingen, eleventh century mystic, who referred to this type of environment as *viriditas* or greening power, where "the earth sweats germinating power from its very pores." She compared this to when she heard God speak:

I am the breeze that nurtures all things green.

I encourage blossoms to flourish with ripening fruits.

I am the rain coming from the dew

that causes the grasses to laugh

with the joy of life.

I was even happy to drive into our cul-de-sac and see the neighborhood children swarming the street, riding their tricycles, throwing baseballs, and swinging their bats. Marissa's sixth birthday was around the corner on June 10. All these neighborhood friends would soon be receiving an invitation for her big celebration. A few days later, when I ordered Marissa's birthday cake, I made sure her favorite doll, Strawberry Shortcake, was replicated with frosting on the cake. Our daughter's birthday was going to be extra special in light of the Black Madonna's prediction. I tried really hard not to dwell on the dark side of it.

Marissa sat with her presents in the center of the family room as her friends, bubbling with laughter, encircled her. I stood against the door and marveled at the sheer joy in the heart of a child. Eventually, the children's enthusiasm overflowed into the backyard where the partygoers pushed each other on the swings and down the slide. After the party ended, Marissa and Andrea played with the new toys until bedtime.

My daily life slipped into "business as usual." Our marriage picked up where we left off. Mark left for work in the wee hours of the morning. I awoke Marissa and Andrea and got them ready for school. After I dropped them off, I drove home, cleaned the house, and returned my clients' messages.

One day, as I was putting the dishes into the dishwasher, I felt like someone was in the kitchen watching over me, even in this most ordinary household chore. I stood quietly, listening and feeling. Who could this be? Then I felt a motherly tender warmth. Even though I was unable to see her, I knew this loving presence was the Black Madonna.

"I thought I had left you in Einsiedeln," I mumbled.

I was surprised, but happy that I felt her warmth once again. I realized she was now a part of me, and she would be with me no matter where I lived. I rarely talked to anyone about Einsiedeln, mostly because I lacked the understanding to describe the Madonna's presence that I felt intuitively. But I knew I had to honor the beauty of our relationship in some way. I was eager to see her in my physical world, like in a painting hanging in my living room, so I could gaze at her beautiful dark face. I regretted not bringing a statue or picture of her from Switzerland. I wondered where I could find one in Seattle.

Our Lady of Guadalupe was the only other dark Madonna I knew. Over 500 years ago, Our Lady appeared to the peasant, Juan Diego, during some of the most tumultuous times in Mexican history when the Spaniards murdered thousands of indigenous Indians and Mexicans. Our Lady gave instructions for Juan Diego to build a church on Tepeyac Hill, a site where Aztec earth goddesses were worshipped. She left her indigenous portrait, the only time the Virgin Mary has provided an image of herself, imprinted on Juan Diego's *tilma* (cloak) as proof to the bishop of her message. And in the process, Our Lady was embedded in the soul of the Mexican culture. The cloak is enshrined in the Basilica de Nuestra Señora de Guadalupe in Mexico City where millions of women and men experience her divine maternal love. Her devotees traveled north into the southwestern states of New Mexico and Colorado. So special Our Lady of Guadalupe was to the Indians and to the Mexicans and to the women of my own family, that I knew my relationship with the Black Madonna would be equally important.

One day as I was reviewing my clients' files, Mark telephoned. "Hi, I just wanted you to know that I have several business trips lined up. And Dan and I are thinking about that trip to Alaska. We'll be gone for about a week."

"Sounds exciting. While you're in Alaska would you mind looking for a painting of the Black Madonna? I can't find one here. I have an inkling that the once-Russian territory might have her."

"Sure."

Shortly after Mark returned from his Alaskan trip, a large rectangular box arrived at the house. I carried the brown package upstairs, laid it on the bed, cut the tape off, and unfolded layer upon layer of bubble wrap. A porous black frame appeared before my eyes. In the black and brown paint, I saw a woman with big brown eyes holding a child on her lap. Both figures wore Russian fur caps circled with golden halos. The woman appeared as a shadow against a gold background. "Oh my God, it's my precious Black Madonna!"

Mark ran upstairs and was excited to share the details of his treasure hunt. "When Dan and I arrived in Anchorage, we searched the shops. I was almost ready to give up, but I returned to an art gallery that I had visited earlier. To my surprise, an icon of the Black Madonna had just been placed on the wall. I had to buy it on the spot. The gallery owner had purchased the painting at an estate sale in San Francisco from a Koski family who had owned it since the turn of the century."

I leaned over and kissed him. "Thank you so much."

"I know how important the Madonna is to you, so I kept looking for her."

I placed the icon in the entrance hall of our home. A friend, who was a Greek Orthodox priest, examined the icon and found "Roma-1736" hidden in the Madonna's headdress.

Above her head, written in old Greek, were the words "Mother of God."

The only thing I knew about this painting was that it radiated holiness. Leonid Ouspensky and Vladimir Lossky's book, *The Meaning of Icons*, became my teacher as if I were its only student in the lecture hall. The authors spoke to me in their writings: "The icon never strives to stir the emotions of the faithful. Its task is not to provoke in them one or another natural human emotion, but to guide every emotion as well as the reason and all the other faculties of human nature on the way towards transfiguration."

The authors continued, "If an icon is authentic, the iconographer will not sign his work, because he believes that the image comes from God." They explained that the iconographer's spiritual discipline of prayer and fasting revealed the image. I decided that this icon was the perfect guide in understanding the Black Madonna. In order to grow in this relationship, I needed to establish a spiritual discipline similar to the iconographer.

Already, when I prayed and meditated, I felt the Madonna's presence. When I was too busy to attain mindfulness, her presence accumulated into a heaviness, as if I were carrying a ten-pound backpack. But when I sat down and became quiet and prayed, I discovered what was in the backpack, whether it was insights, inspiration, or ideas. The more I meditated, the less I felt this heaviness, as if meditation helped me to embody her wisdom. In her world of silence and darkness, I was able to listen to her.

The million-dollar question was: where was I going to find time in my busy life style to develop a more serious contemplative discipline?

In reality, this practice collided with my deep-rooted daily routine. In the past, as crazy as it sounded, my goal was to accomplish the most in the shortest period of time. It was as if my personal worth was dependent on how busy I was, even if I was stressed-out and robbed of all my energy. Any extra time I had disappeared in returning telephone calls, driving in rush hour, and waiting in line at the supermarket. And this was hard enough for me before the onset of the technological age of cell phones, iPad, and laptop computers with email, Facebook, Twitter, and other distractions.

One typical morning, I was getting ready for work, and I had to drop Marissa and Andrea at the babysitter. Mark was on another business trip.

"Hurry, hurry." My voice was impatient and abrupt.

Marissa ran to the playroom to find her Strawberry Shortcake doll, and Andrea gathered her Little Ponies as fast as she could. As my demanding words left my tongue, I reprimanded myself: *What am I teaching my darling children—to rush at everything they do, so they can live in a constant state of anxiety? Why am I always racing around like a maniac? What is wrong with me?* I was changing inside, and now my outer life had to reflect this inner transformation. The routine I was accustomed to no longer served my needs.

Marissa and Andrea's childlike ways of capturing stillness by playing with their toys, enjoying the delight of eating a ripened tomato like an apple, and gathering a bouquet of dandelions were also teaching me to *s l o w   d o w n.* How could I practice mindfulness if I was always driving in the express lane? I had to switch to the slow lane rather than demand that they drive with me at breakneck speed. I had so much to learn from Marissa and Andrea's ability to live in the present. My children were my teachers in how to exist fully in the moment.

Clearly, I needed a chopping board to cut out my nonessential activities and then learn how to prioritize the rest. Mark was in his own world of the computer company and was oblivious to how I was trying to change my life. This was not going to be easy. But I had renewed clarity, like wearing new corrective lenses. I was determined to make the necessary changes so that I would have time for a relationship with the Black Madonna.

Watching television and my favorite soap opera, *The Young and The Restless,* and other shows were eliminated. Most television shows promoted a narrow perspective rather than offering stimulating ideas. Now, behavior on sitcoms appeared abusive and contrary to the life of compassion. I observed how television promoted consumerism, a myth that the quality of my life was dependent on how many new vehicles and technological gadgets I bought.

On the other hand, I devoured books on meditation and spiritual lives, like the passionate Spanish Saint Teresa of Avila, thirteenth-century Rumi, Yogananda, and other mystics who plunged into the fires of transformation. Rarely did I hear language on television that compared to the words of Saint John of the Cross:

I remained lost in oblivion;

My face I reclined on the Beloved.

All ceased and I abandoned myself,

Leaving my cares forgotten among the lilies.

Surprisingly, once I set meditation as a priority, the process gave me freedom. I felt like I had been a caged bird finally released into the sky. Attending classes on mindfulness was not necessary. I just needed the discipline and devotion to quiet my life. Even with my responsibilities as a mother and a wife, I grabbed opportunities for time alone, whether it was at midnight or three o'clock in the morning. Sometimes, after I dropped off Marissa and Andrea at their Montessori school, I returned to our quiet house where I could meditate for an hour before I left for work.

I began my spiritual discipline by first lighting a candle. For me, this symbolized the Divine Light that sparks illumination, new insights, and novel ideas. Then I sat in a comfortable chair that fully supported my body. Because of my Catholic background, I chose the rosary and its repetitive prayers and sounds, similar to prayer beads that many Hindus, Muslims, and Buddhists also use to reach this meditative state. Oftentimes, a CD of Gregorian chants and their melodies led me into this inner refuge, a place that reminded me of the meadow full of daisies where the Black Madonna was waiting to embrace me— a place where I was fed and strengthened, similar to a wildlife refuge that sustains birds and animals in their migratory journey.

No other daily routine captured the Black Madonna's presence as deeply as this meditative state. The Madonna loved me without any judgments. She held me, similar to a baby, in her intuitive world. Her compassion was like having a warm soft flannel blanket thrown around me, and then she pulled me close to her where I heard the rhythm of her loving heart.

In this inner place, calm enveloped me like an ocean mist until I was less here and more there, while images appeared then disappeared. Sometimes, feelings surfaced. I felt them, and then they fluttered away. At times, a clarity of thought or a sense of peacefulness seeped through me. Meditation was like being tucked in the eye of a hurricane—hiding in a tiny pocket of serenity while the chaos of daily life flew around me. In this suspended state, thoughts emerged within me: *In silence, the seed of the self, momentarily detached from the demands of the physical world, drops into the rich dark soil of the intuitive and sprouts wisdom in the morning light.*

I slowly returned where I felt the soft cushion underneath me. Afterwards, I took this contentment and peacefulness into my personal and professional relationships. Occasionally, when I lacked the time to meditate, I reverted to that familiar place on the fast track where I forgot to be loving and to live with an open heart. I failed to be patient with my children and friends, and I rushed at decisions.

Over the following months, I continued this meditative practice in which my relationship with the Madonna unfolded. She had few requirements, but she did demand that I live in the present. Yesterdays and tomorrows were simply irrelevant. This blessed moment was all that was real and important.

No matter what feelings I carried, they never overwhelmed her. My emotions were the vessel where I experienced the Madonna. She valued them, and they served as a means to communicate with her and with myself. Over time, I became more accepting of my anger, my disappointments, and my sadness. These emotions fed, strengthened, and protected me.

I had to listen to their knowledge. They were just a part of living. I was no longer a spectator that only observed what was happening around me; now I had reactions and input.

Our meditative relationship was like an osmosis where I absorbed the Madonna's love and compassion, then I shared this love with people around me. When I interacted with friends and family, I strove to be emotionally transparent. When I disagreed with their ideas, I simply said, "I just want to share how I'm feeling about this." My desire was to be real and present without any need for their acceptance or agreement with my ideas.

Because of my relationship with the Black Madonna, I became intimately connected to everything and everyone in the universe. For example, when I saw children in church, I was drawn to connect with them by smiling or by tapping the top of their heads. I felt empathy with their parents. I knew raising children was hard and self-sacrificing.

One time we were shopping in Safeway when Andrea grabbed a bag of her favorite candy, Skittles.

I returned the bag to the shelf and said, "No, you can't have any candy now." She screamed so loudly that I had to throw her over my shoulder, abandon my shopping cart, and walk out of the store. Sometimes, it was difficult to set limits with my girls. Yet because I was loved by the Madonna, I had the confidence to set boundaries with others while appreciating the full spectrum of human behavior.

I felt like a child of Nature, especially when we returned to Colorado to spend time with family during vacations and holidays, which was several times a year. In contrast to Seattle's cloudy weather and bright city lights, Colorado's skies were clear and expansive. At night, the crisp mountain air that wafted through the window screen wrapped me in its freshness while the full moon grabbed my pillow. I lay awake staring at the Milky Way that stretched across the universe while the stars winked at me. I gazed at the moon for hours, captivated by her constancy and fullness of light.

With this new consciousness, I thought about Einsiedeln when the Black Madonna told me that she was going to take Marissa. I now understood that she wanted to take "the Marissa," the child within me that she had embraced in her arms. And, as my Divine Mother, she was teaching me about the world of the Feminine, beginning with the importance of our relationship and my relationships with others. This new awareness was changing the course of my life.

Chapter Five

CHAKRAS IN THE SUBTLE BODY

The Black Madonna's archetypal energy had seized my psyche and had pierced every cell of my being. This time my body was not awakened by a high school sweetheart or by menstrual pain, but by another source. When I first felt a sensation streaming from my torso to the top of my head, I knew I was connected to something primordial.

Decades ago as an adolescent, I had disowned my body and with it my sexuality. My body brought pain, confusion, and challenges that ultimately served as a wall of bricks that separated my neck from the rest of my frame. I had thought that being pregnant—an intimate connection to my body—and delivering my daughters would change my perspective. But no solitary experience could accomplish that. My formative years greatly contributed to this complex issue.

Mom's upbringing about the dichotomy of women who were either good or bad complicated this issue. Sometimes Mom pointed to certain women whom she labeled as *mujeres buenas* (good women) or *mujeres malas* (bad women) without an explanation. With a gruff intonation when she said *malas*, I knew I better not be known as that person. It was all about sexuality, which Mom refused to discuss with me. If I had asked, "Mom, what do you mean by a bad woman?" Her response would have been, "Shh, don't talk back to me." I grew up in an era when parents were not questioned and during a time when women were polarized. If I wanted to be known as a respected lady, I believed, I had to disown my sexuality.

To further complicate this issue, when I was seven years old, I had some confusing experiences with men. Often, I was afraid to go to my bedroom alone. I liked Daddy's reassurance when he carried me and tucked me into my twin bed. One time after Daddy left, a male relative who was visiting somehow ended up sitting at the foot of my bed. He looked short and thin like a silhouette. I was confused about his presence, which scared me. Finally, he left, and I fell asleep.

When I was a teenager, another incident happened when I slept at a cousin's house. Late in the night I heard my cousin's husband walk into my bedroom. He continued his pace to the window at the end of the room. I pretended I was asleep after I wrapped the blankets around my neck. He left my room, and, again, later in the night he returned and stood by the window. I was perplexed about why he was in my room so late at night. Was he waiting for someone, or was he getting ready to pounce on me? Finally, he left the room. Without saying a word to anyone, I found the incident so odd that I never felt safe around him again.

Also, as an adolescent, my relationship with my body was influenced by my severe monthly menstrual cramps. Why was I born in a body that caused me so much despair? In order to survive for those few days, I stayed in bed or attended classes while trying to tolerate the pain.

In high school my hormones were troublemakers. I dated John, an upperclassman who was intelligent, good-looking, and kind and who asked me to prom. After the dance, we cuddled and kissed in his car. Slowly, he maneuvered his clothed body on top of me. The pressure of his body was just too much for this Catholic girl. It seemed like my long prom dress was getting shorter by the second, and I was feeling like I had eaten jalapeño peppers. I wanted him in a sexual way that I never could have imagined. It took all my willpower to come up for air. With more oxygen in my brain, I was able to think about not wanting to disappoint my parents. And I refused to be a bad example for my little sisters. The next few kisses were our last. (Well, maybe it was more than just a *few* kisses.)

Sunday Mass only instilled so much willpower in me. I was confused about how to handle my sexual passions; so, to make things easier, I ended the relationship with John by dating another upperclassman who—I was confident— would not trigger these overwhelming impulses.

Somehow in college it was easier to make decisions based on what I wanted rather than what was expected of me. Fort Collins was about 300 miles away from home, but it felt more like 3,000 miles. When I fell deeply in love with Mark, I thought sexual intimacy was the next progression in our relationship. Daddy recognized how serious Mark and I were becoming. When I flew to Arizona to visit Mark, Daddy advised, "Be careful who you give your heart to." And we both knew what he meant by "heart."

At first, Mark and I enjoyed the excitement of love and sexual intimacy. But in our marriage, as the stress increased, we had less time for each other. My only recourse was to suppress my sexual impulses, along with their physical energy and the instincts they carried. My need to express my sexuality went into hibernation for years.

On the contrary, in Einsiedeln the Black Madonna was dynamic in her sexuality. She looked alive and regal as she stood like a queen in a Spanish court, dressed in a red and gold garment crowned with a gold tiara. She was a woman who even preferred wearing dangling earrings.

The combination of the Madonna's womanliness and her divinity gave birth to Jesus Christ, whom she was holding in her left arm. During Roman times, Jesus brought radical ideas of treating men and women with honorable love.

After the Madonna's embrace, like a volcano spewing

hot lava, a new consciousness was forming. The Madonna's presence was activating strange electric charges, similar to static, throughout my body. It was like a fire was burning within me. Meditation was fanning this fire while the heat was causing sparks of awareness. Meditation was helping to integrate and embody this Feminine energy while, at the same time, it was fueling this electric current. More times than not, I was scared about what was happening to my body.

But this was only the beginning. A few weeks after I returned from Switzerland, I was visiting my neighbor Mara Lou. In her kitchen while we drank coffee and laughed and talked, I suddenly felt a bee flying through my thick hair. "Mara Lou, what's in my hair?"

She sensed my urgency, so she used her fingers to comb through my curls. "There's nothing there," she said.

I shook my head like a dust mop. Surprisingly, nothing flew out. "Mara Lou, I swear it feels like bees swarming through my hair."

We continued talking, and I continued feeling this moving sensation.

"I'm sorry. I have to walk home. Whatever is going on in my head is too distracting." I poured my coffee down the sink and left for home, which was only a block away.

With each step the bee sensation intensified until, by the time I unlocked the front door, I felt thousands of bees swarming through my hair. I grabbed a hairbrush and combed my hair, but not one bee or spider or any insect flew out. Okay, by now I thought, *I'm going nuts.* The word "panic" failed to capture my situation. Maybe "terror" or maybe all these words together: I was in a terrifying, horrific panic!

Suddenly an image flashed in my inner eye: *I'm jumping into a bathtub of water, head and all.* With that inspiration, I ran upstairs, filled the tub with water, tore my clothes off, and slid under the water, head and all. When I finally lifted my sopping hair, I saw in my inner eye an image of Christ in prayer in the Garden of Gethsemane. The annoying stimulation on top of my head was gone. I failed to spend time reflecting on this image of Christ, because I was overwhelmed with joy that the bee sensation had finally disappeared. Thank you, God!

During the following months the bee sensation returned, but this time it covered my entire body. I felt nausea, like in my first trimester of pregnancy. In retrospect, I was pregnant, but this time spiritually. At first, food was just too much. When I was able to eat, I preferred light food such as vegetables, fruit, fish, little meat, and lots of water. High fatty caloric food seemed to overload my new delicate system.

Another remarkable sensation began with heat on my skin, localized at the base of my spine and then traveling upward. The intense warmth made me want to constantly scratch my back. At times, my bones and muscles ached, which required that I take naps. Without any questions, my family accepted that I needed this additional rest.

I might have rested, but that did not stop me from searching for answers and understanding of this bewildering phenomenon that oftentimes left me in a panic. Luckily, I discovered Louis Vuksinick, who was a contributor to *The Sacred Heritage*. Vuksinick wrote:

> In Buddhist tradition, the 'subtle body' is portrayed as having seven centers of energy. They are called chakras and are depicted as wheels that ascend up the middle of the body from the pelvis to the crown of the head. Kundalini, symbolized as a snake and representing female energy, is the force that, when awakened, activates these chakras from below, moving energy from one chakra to the next toward higher consciousness.

Vuksinick gave me the paradigm that I was desperately searching for.

In Hinduism and Buddhism, this universal energy or breath and spirit are referred to as *Atma* and *Prana*. Yogis tap into this force through breathing techniques, meditation, and physical exercise that elevate them to a higher state of consciousness. The Chinese believe that all matter is composed of this universal vital life force energy which they call *Chi*, and in Judaism it is called *Ruach*. In Western Christianity, this breath is known as the Holy Spirit. I remembered in my adolescence when the bishop laid his hands on the crown of my head and said, "*Accipe signaculum doni Spiritus Sancti.*" (Be sealed with the Gift of the Holy Spirit.) The Black Madonna had triggered the chakras in my subtle body, thus releasing this stream of energy.

I also found Jungian psychology extremely helpful. From a Jungian perspective, the Black Madonna was referred to as an archetype, meaning universal patterns with psychic energy that produce monumental consequences. Jung cautioned, "It is a great mistake in practice to treat an archetype as if it were a mere name, word, or concept. It is far more than that: it is a piece of life, an image connected with the living individual by the bridge of emotion." I could attest that the Black Madonna was much more than a theoretical concept. She was dynamic, and her Feminine force streamed through my physical body. In my vision, when the Black Madonna embraced me, I never saw the Madonna's face. A dark hood covered it, which emphasized her universality rather than her individuality. For all men and women, she was an aspect of their psyches. I concluded that these spiritual traditions and the Jungian perspective all referred to the same universal source.

During this Kundalini process, I avoided going through it alone. It would have been like trying to control a field of fire in fifty-mile-per-hour winds without asking for help. I leaned on my psychoanalyst and friends who understood the chakra system and its implications. I also found homeopathic medicine, body work, and acupuncture helpful in integrating this life force.

I learned that my subtle body, which had always overlapped my physical body, is composed of chakras or energy wheels. When opened, they released a force onto my physical body. Seven major chakras, with a constant interplay of energy, were activated by this female Kundalini that had been triggered by the Black Madonna's embrace.

I imagined these chakras as a string of Christmas lights with seven bulbs superimposed on my physical body. And when one bulb is not glowing, it affects the entire string of lights. The first light sits at the base of my spine with each light ascending up my back until the last bulb sits at the crown of my head. Some of these lights or chakras were already lit while others were flipped on by the Black Madonna.

The first bulb or chakra's energy is associated with the physical world of earth, food, and survival and serves as the foundation for the rest of the chakras. Like gravity, this chakra pulls me toward the earth and keeps me rooted to the material world. This is extremely important, because it allows me to ascend to a higher consciousness or awareness while I remain grounded in my physicality.

This first chakra must have already been opened, because,

after my encounter with the Black Madonna, there was not a shift in this area of my body. Understandably so, since I had always been well-connected to the earth. As a child, no matter what I confronted, I always found solace and comfort playing in the alfalfa and lying on the grass as I watched the chameleon-like clouds. As an adult, I loved being outdoors, walking on the beach on the Oregon coast, and burying my feet in the wet sand.

Moving upward to the second light bulb, the second chakra is situated in the lower abdomen between the navel and genitals. This chakra is referred to as the "seat of life," the center for sexuality. It is also associated with pleasure and emotions. My second chakra was opened after the Madonna embraced me while we stood in the meadow of daisies. I knew when this opened, because I felt as if a dam had burst. No surprise since I always had difficulty connecting with my sexuality, and I was oblivious to my emotions. Sometimes, it took over twenty-four hours for me to realize what I was feeling.

In the past, I was most comfortable discussing ideas, organization, and activities while I tended to pack away my feelings with the rest of my personal belongings. What an illusion! Now, I was forced to unpack my emotions, which eventually proved to be my greatest assets.

This chakra or center of sexuality sometimes overwhelmed me with its energy. Out of desperation, I learned how to control this chakra by placing wrapped ice packs against my hot skin, which brought relief. To balance this energy, I sprayed witch hazel—a liquid distilled from this plant's leaves, bark, and twigs—on the bottoms of my feet. I purchased witch hazel at the local pharmacy or at the health food store. I also found traditional cold showers and soaking in bathwater with drops of lavender oil helpful. Burying my feet in the sandy beach while cold ocean water splashed over them was beneficial, but the ocean was not always accessible to me. Closer to home, gardening and pulling weeds released this energy into the soil.

The third chakra, located below the sternum and extending to the navel, is referred to as the solar plexus. It brings fire, warmth, and personal power into the human being and is associated with will and self-esteem. With the Black Madonna's support, I now possessed an incredible amount of confidence that I had rarely felt in my life. I felt empowered to deal with any situation that I was confronted with.

The fourth chakra, referred to as the heart chakra, corresponds to love, relationships, and healing. This chakra serves as the central point to the chakra system and spiritual center. The confluence of energy from below and from above is a meeting point for both spirit and matter. According to Jung, individuation is manifested when there is a total purification of the subtle body chakras and when Kundalini pierces and activates the heart chakra. In other words, an opened heart was the only way for me to reach my fullest potential.

Now I could see clearly with the eyes of my heart. I felt a connectedness with all humanity instead of seeing our differences. And being a woman held a special meaning. When I saw other pregnant women, I felt a camaraderie with them and shared in their joys of motherhood as well as in its challenges. As parents, we shared the responsibilities for loving, nurturing, and educating *all* our children.

The fifth chakra, associated with communication, sound, and creativity, is situated in the throat. As a child, my perceptions only got me in trouble, especially with Vivien and Veronica. As an adult, I felt safer in intellectual discussions about philosophy or psychology. But when it came time to share my feelings, the fortress walls appeared. After this communication chakra was awakened, I realized that listening to my perceptions was crucial, not only as a psychotherapist, but in my personal relationships. I learned how to listen to family and friends while valuing their words and their experiences. Using the lame excuse that I was too busy or just giving the impression that I was fully present was unacceptable. This relationship was a two-way street, in which I wanted the same respect and the same understanding I was giving them.

The sixth chakra—or third eye—sits in the indentation between the eyebrows and is the center for intuition. I remembered when I was in Zürich talking to my student-therapist and telling him what the Madonna had said, it had felt as if a fist were making its way through the dimple of my forehead.

Thankfully, within seconds the pain was gone and only a soreness remained. Weeks later during final exams, I became aware of this intuitive knowledge, especially when the answers instantly came to me. The Black Madonna uses intuition as a means of communication. A relationship with the Feminine requires a relationship with the intuitive. Examples of my intuition were when an image spontaneously appeared, when I felt a strong feeling about a situation, or when I intuitively felt the Madonna's love. I found myself continually integrating these intuitive experiences.

The seventh chakra, situated on the top of the head, illuminates understanding and spiritual wisdom. I felt this opening on the crown of my head when I felt hundreds of bees flying through my hair while I was visiting my friend Mara Lou. After jumping into a bathtub full of water, which was inspired by an image, I was able to ground this spiritual energy. This tickling sensation on the top of my head that traveled upward into the air continues to this day. Instead of feeling panicked, I smile as if God is saying, "You are not alone. I am always with you."

Finding words to describe the opening of my chakras was challenging. It was similar to describing an experience of a nine-point-zero earthquake. I attempted to explain my intense fear and the magnitude of living through a major shift in my psyche and in my body. But the more I tried to bring logic and understanding to the chakra system, the more my experiences lost their potency and were no longer in the dynamic here and now. It was hard to explain the power of the experience and the difficulty of the process. But the process was worth it, as my chakras would come to play an essential role in my creative work that was waiting for me on the horizon.

Chapter Six

The Feast of the Miraculous Consecration of the Black Madonna

In Seattle on a brisk September morning, I drove to church. I knelt on the fabric-covered pew cushion, waiting for Sunday Mass to begin.

The priest walked into the sanctuary and commenced, "In the name of the Father, the Son, and the Holy Spirit."

As the priest was praying, I heard music as if angels were singing. Gregorian chants with their deep prolonged melodies echoed in my ears. I looked for the church choir, but I was unable to find the singers or the origin of these glorious sounds. Inwardly, the chanting served as a magic carpet that took me to Einsiedeln and to the Feast of the Miraculous Consecration of the Black Madonna. However, at the time, my rational mind did not know that the Madonna's feast day was the following day, September 14. Intuitively, the information came to me as naturally as the numbers one plus one equals two. Mass ended, and while driving home on the winding road, I thought about how exciting to stand next to the altar of the Black Madonna in Einsiedeln once again.

But cold reality from my rational mind snapped me out of my bliss.

What an absolutely crazy idea. It was out of the question. How could I possibly be in Switzerland within twenty-four hours in order to participate in this feast day? I had just been there about a year ago.

To appease my logical mind and to confirm this intuitive impulse, I telephoned the Benedictine monastery in Einsiedeln when I returned home.

An English-speaking monk confirmed my prescience. "Yes, the Feast of the Miraculous Consecration of the Black Madonna is set for tomorrow."

I was stunned! Knowing the answers to the tests while studying in Zürich was one thing, but the date of the celebration intuitively coming forth made me pause. Wow! I was learning that these spontaneous impulses that were completely out of my control were like intuitive lightning bolts.

I decided not to let my rational mind discourage me. I called the airlines. The only flight to Zürich was scheduled to leave within three hours. "Mark, I don't know what to do."

"You're only going to be away for forty-eight hours. Marissa and Andrea will be going to school, then daycare.

Then, I'll pick them up after work. You'll be home before you know it."

I grabbed the telephone, called Swiss Air, and made a reservation.

I ran upstairs to pack my passport in the overnight bag. First, in an effort to slow the pace of this trip, I fanned the pages of my passport. Stamps printed at Rome, Munich, and Athens flew by. I continued gathering my makeup and nightgown. When it came time to leave, my doubts, coupled with fear, were so heavy that I was unable to pick up my overnight bag and walk downstairs to the foyer. This was not complicated. I lacked the strength to travel so far away and this time all by myself. My last trip to Zürich was so much easier, because I had months to prepare, and I was traveling with friends. Plus, now I was having difficulty justifying spending thousands of dollars for a two-day trip.

I looked at the clock on the nightstand. I was fretting so much that now I was late for the plane. I burst into tears. I was so torn between ignoring this experience or trusting this unfamiliar spontaneity that required a snap-of-the-fingers response, leaving me little time to prepare my rational mind. No doubt I wanted to be a participant at the Black Madonna's festivities, but I needed more time to prepare my family and me. However, if I wanted to be in Einsiedeln, I needed to leave right *now*.

I ran downstairs to talk with Mark. He was drinking coffee when he looked up with a matter-of-fact suggestion, "Call Swiss Air to see if the flight left."

I picked up the phone. "I would like to know if the 2:00 p.m. flight to Zürich has left?"

"No. It's been delayed," said the agent.

A jolt of adrenaline shot through me. I had a second chance. "I have a reservation. I'm only twenty minutes away from the airport. Is it possible to get on that flight?"

"Yes. Go directly to the gate, and your ticket will be waiting for you."

Mark parked the car at the airport's curb. He turned and put his arms around me. "Breathe. You're going to be okay. I love you." Then he kissed me.

"I love you, too." I turned to the backseat where Marissa and Andrea sat. "I love you girls. Take good care of Daddy, and he's going to take good care of you. I love you all." I jumped out of the car. I ran through Sea-Tac Airport to the international terminal. This was prior to the 9/11 terrorist attacks, so a boarding pass was not required to reach the terminal.

"Why is this flight delayed?" asked another passenger who had walked off the plane.

The agent looked at my ticket as he spoke, "Sir, we'll be departing immediately."

Once on board I slipped into my seat and scanned the Boeing 747 that was as big as a gymnasium. I could barely breathe or move, as if I were frozen in a block of ice. I had jumped out of my comfort zone and followed my intuition. I could not bring any logic to this expensive short trip. I tried to comfort myself:

Listening to my inner knowing is as important as working with my intellect. I need to trust this information originating from my third eye chakra and include it in my decision-making process. I'm simply following the Black Madonna. Yes, I'm physically by myself, but the Black Madonna is with me. No matter where I am, she is my invisible companion who will always protect me. My spiritual journey is priceless. And it can't be valued in dollars and cents.

Then a peaceful feeling washed over me, as if I heard her voice, "Abandon all fear. Enrapture yourself in trust." And with those words, I nuzzled into my blanket for the nine-hour flight.

After I arrived in Zürich, I rode the shuttle to the main train station, Zürich Hauptbahnhof. As I waited, I looked at the round vintage-like clock. Over a year ago, my friends and I must have glanced at that clock a hundred times while waiting for the trains to Lake Geneva, Lugano, Lucerne, and the Swiss capitol, Bern. I hopped on the train, and without knowing any details of the celebration, I arrived in Einsiedeln.

The church bells were ringing loudly, heavy metal

pounding against metal that sounded like an instrument from antiquity. On this cool autumn day, the town was brimming with crowds of pilgrims. I was so excited to see the shrine of the Black Madonna again. When I saw the towering Benedictine monastery, I wanted to run but reined in my pace when I saw hundreds of people congregated in small groups and others meandering through the plaza.

When I entered the church, I dipped my fingers in the font of holy water. I made the Sign of the Cross, feeling drops of holy water blessing me and wrapping me with the Father, the Son, and the Holy Spirit. I looked up at the Baroque architecture and noticed those sweet angels holding blue and peach ribbons as if they were on their way to decorate the Lady's chapel. I wanted to pinch their rosy cheeks like my daughters', but instead I found my way through the crowd to the chapel.

It was as if I were seeing the Madonna for the first time. Last time, I was caught in an avalanche of emotions after she said, "I'm going to take Marissa." Her words had paralyzed me while her altar, the church, and the pilgrims melted into oblivion.

This time I was the observer, watching and examining her altar. While I gazed at her wooden figure, I focused on her delicate face and hands, and then I saw the Baby Jesus in her left arm and noticed a bird sitting in Jesus's hand. I was taken aback by all their blackness, still so unfamiliar to me. At the same time, she captured my curiosity. She wore an ornamental gold robe with a crown on her head, and in her right hand, she held a gold scepter like a queen reigning with absolute authority. The last time I saw her, the Madonna's robe was red, an indication of how her cloth robe is changed according to the liturgical season. Now, it looked as if she had stepped out of brilliant gold clouds with bolts of intuitive lightning behind her.

I realized that her regal authority, which was complemented by her innocence and purity, preserved ancient truths. There was no past that robbed the blessings from the present nor did the unknowns of the future infringe upon this blessed moment.

I found an empty space in a wooden pew in front of the Madonna's altar. Hundreds of men and women, young and old, prayed in reverence to their Divine Mother. As a man left the church, he turned and blew her a kiss, as if saying farewell to his beloved. A Swiss woman with a handkerchief in her hand was wiping tears from her rosy cheeks. An older man was spontaneously leading songs in a loud deep voice that was expressing his love for this sacred woman bathed in black. Her mysterious darkness radiated intimacy and oneness with everyone in the church as if she were a hearth whose warmth drew everyone near her.

Unexpectedly, my observations were interrupted by

loud voices. Four gray-haired Swiss women whispered among themselves. They pointed to an elderly man. I interpreted through their gestures that, when one of the women had left her seat, the man had sat in it. When she returned, he refused to relinquish her seat. The woman was like a mother bear ready to attack him. The man sat calmly and defiantly, saying with his body language that he was there to stay and no person in this church, not even these assertive Swiss women, were going to force him to leave. Indeed, this Black Madonna creates enduring loyalty and devotion.

The night of the Feast of the Miraculous Consecration culminated in a candlelit processional led by the Benedictine monks. These holy men, dressed in brown cassocks and with their eyes cast downward, shuffled in unison toward Our Lady's Chapel. They stood in front of the chapel in two rows and then lifted their eyes to the Black Madonna. In Latin they chanted:

Salve, Regina, mater misericordiae; vita, dulcedo et spes nosta, salve.

(Hail, Holy Queen, mother of mercy; our life, our sweetness and our hope, hail.)

I closed my eyes and followed the elongated sounds until they lifted me into the celestial clouds where I was one with my God. I simply floated on the monks' symphony of devotion and love to their *Mutter Maria hilt mir.* These deep prolonged

Gregorian chants were exactly what I had heard at Mass in Seattle. Here, it was not necessary to search for their source. I simply absorbed this sacred music.

I had never witnessed men honor a woman with such reverence. Perhaps, when men and women honor their Feminine qualities of intuition and spirituality, they are able to sing these hymns of holiness. Did these prayerful men feel that the Divine Feminine made them complete? Earlier, a monk who was limping and walking with a cane opened the gate to the Madonna's altar. The monk's lips smiled as if he knew this secret.

I was so deeply touched by this sacred ritual and the monks' reverence to their beloved that I felt tears in my eyes. In America, such devotion to the Feminine was a rarity. In Great Britain, the British have their beloved Queen Elizabeth II. No matter what their opinions are of the monarch, the queen serves as a visible reminder of the Feminine. In the United States for the general population, there are few images of the Feminine. Of course a person will find her image in churches and in such places like New York City's Statue of Liberty, who welcomes immigrants to their new homeland. In America, sometimes the brilliance of the mind is honored and celebrated with graduation parties and expensive gifts; the power of the ego and all its achievements sometimes overshadows the magnificent legacy of the spiritual that is elevated with rituals and traditions.

The monks shuffled their sandals against the marble floor. They merged into a recessional line led by pilgrims and children who carried bundles of wild flowers wrapped in long pink and green ribbons. While they were walking through the front doors, some pilgrims held long, lighted, cream-colored candles. I followed the recessional as they left the church into the night with the darkness of the distant forest behind them.

I remembered reading about this *finsterwald* (the forest) in Fred Gustafson's *The Black Madonna of Einsiedeln, An Ancient Image for Our Present Time*. According to legend, over a thousand years earlier, Saint Meinrad lived beneath these stars and moon and rested on a bed of fir needles and branches with spidery ferns tickling his nose. Living within this mysterious canopy of trees, Saint Meinrad was a long way from his aristocratic upbringing in the castle of his ancestors, the Counts of Hohenzöllern.

At age twenty-five, Saint Meinrad had been ordained a Benedictine priest and was known for his scholarly and business acuity. He was sent to teach at Benken, located in upper Lake Zürich where the Benedictines had started a school.

At age thirty-one, he began a life of solitude in his self-made hermitage on Etzel Mountain. His reputation for holiness spread, and villagers continually visited him. He was drawn into a deeper life of solitude, prayer, and fasting and withdrew farther into the forest across the Sihl River, taking the Rule of

Saint Benedict and a statue of the Virgin Mary—which became the Black Madonna of Einsiedeln—with him. The damp thick forest might have felt imposing for some people, but for Saint Meinrad, it was an invitation to live life differently, to surrender to the Spirit. In this place, the Feminine, also referred to as Our Lady of the Hermits, fed him spiritually while he developed his saintly qualities. Einsiedeln means "the hermitage."

When Saint Meinrad entered the *finsterwald,* he heard two hawks flapping their wings as they were attacking a nest of ravens, but he chased the hawks away. Then, he climbed the tree and saved the young birds by feeding and keeping them safe. He built a cell and a chapel there and dedicated it to the Mother of God.

On January 21, 861, Saint Meinrad had a revelation during Mass that he would die that day at the hands of two thieves who were entering the mountain. Disregarding their intent, Saint Meinrad greeted them with food and clothes. Out of nowhere, the men clubbed him to death. When two candles spontaneously lit, the murderers knew they had killed a saint. The murderers fled into town while ravens attacked them. A carpenter at the edge of the forest noticed the chaos, ran into the forest and found Saint Meinrad dead. The two thieves were arrested and condemned to death.

Saint Meinrad had spent twenty-five years living in his humble cell until his death at age sixty-four. The evolution of the Monastery of Einsiedeln began with Saint Meinrad and his relationship with the Virgin Mary. His contemplative life of solitude in the *finsterwald* created this sacred space. In time, other Benedictine monks came to live and pray there. Black ravens in flight became part of the coat of arms for the Benedictine monastery and for the town of Einsiedeln.

Seventy-three years later, Eberhard, a French nobleman, arrived in Einsiedeln where he had drawn plans for a church and a monastery to be built at the exact spot of Meinrad's cell. Upon completion, Eberhard became the first abbot of the Benedictine community, and he wanted the church and the monastery to be blessed.

Eberhard asked Bishop Conrad of Constance to consecrate the holy chapel and the church. Bishop Constance arrived in Einsiedeln on September 14, 948, a day earlier than the scheduled consecration. The stars twinkled in the night sky when the bishop walked into the chapel to pray. Soon he realized that he was not alone. The altar was filled with light and with chants of psalms. He saw Jesus Christ standing in front of the statue of the Virgin Mary with four Evangelists assisting him. Angels were sending incense into the air. Apostles Peter and Paul and Pope Saint Gregory I were present with Saints Augustine and Ambrose.

Later Bishop Conrad explained to Eberhard that he saw Jesus Christ consecrate the chapel, but Eberhard did not believe him. Fred Gustafson wrote, "With great reservation, however, he finally returned to the church at dawn and prepared to ascend the steps leading to the altar in the Holy Chapel, when, as soon as he placed his foot upon the first step of the altar, a seemingly heaven-borne voice was heard by all present: 'Cease brother, the Chapel is divinely consecrated.'"

Gustafson wrote that instead of the church dedicating the chapel *to* the Redeemer, the chapel was dedicated *by* the Redeemer. The Catholic Church honors Saint Conrad on the anniversary of his death on November 26.

As I reflected on this spiritual history, I followed the other pilgrims to the train station from the plaza. If I were going to leave Einsiedeln that night, I needed to be on the last train to Zürich that was scheduled for ten o'clock. I continued to think about Saint Meinrad and his need to withdraw into the forest. I also had withdrawn into meditative prayer as if it were my dark forest. The Feminine was able to emerge and develop into my life as it had in Einsiedeln. I found a seat on the train and returned to Zürich for the night. My plane was set to leave early in the morning for Seattle.

As I deplaned at Sea-Tac Airport, an agent was announcing, "All international passengers must be cleared through customs."

I walked in line and waited my turn to give the uniformed

agent my passport. Finally, she started the interrogation, "How long were you gone?"

"A little over forty-eight hours."

"The purpose of your trip?"

Hmm. . . what should I say? I needed to be truthful, but I was hesitant to tell her about the Black Madonna. Here goes, "I traveled to Switzerland to participate in the celebration of the Miraculous Consecration of the Black Madonna."

The agent grabbed my overnight bag and flipped it upside down. Kathump! All my Swiss chocolate, night gown, and passport tumbled on the table.

I was right. The agent had no idea who the Black Madonna was.

Chapter Seven

Through Dreams: The Evolution of Consciousness

I imagined that Saint Meinrad listened to his dreams while he lived in the *finsterwald* and that imagery and visions were an integral part of his life. Before my encounter with the Black Madonna and prior to my studies in Zürich, dreams and their symbolic language had little value in my personal life. Professionally, I had studied and practiced cognitive and behavioral psychology. But after my first trip to Switzerland, the principles of Jungian psychology greatly influenced my practice and my life.

My inner work was essential, because it gave me a mechanism to see my blind spots. I would be the first person to say that, at times, the unconscious can be brutal and merciless. It could care less whether it made me cry, startled me into 150 heart beats a minute, or sexually excited me. Its goal was to awaken me into wholeness, like a flower that blooms into its fullness.

Psychically, my experience with the Madonna primed me for a committed relationship with symbols that are generated in the unconscious. A dance between the inner world of dreams, images, and intuition and the outer world of relationships, work, and children began with a swirl. The unconscious pushed me along the way with the following dreams.

In the first dream:

October 1, 1987

I see a newspaper with the New York Stock Exchange listing a company that Mark and I have invested in. But the price of the stock is much lower than the current market value and the price we had paid.

Alarmed at the possibility of losing hundreds of thousands of dollars, at breakfast I mentioned the dream to Mark. "I had a dream that the price of our investment drastically dropped. I don't know what to make of it."

Mark sipped the last drop of his coffee. "Oh, that investment is as solid as a rock, but I'll look into it." Later, he said, "I talked to our financial people, and they're not concerned. Even if we could liquidate, we'd have to pay an enormous penalty. I'm not sure that's an option."

"No, we don't have to go that far."

I tried to ignore the dream, but whenever I thought about

it, I became nervous. Sometimes, whispers haunted me: *What if the dream is right? We'll lose hundreds of thousands of dollars.*

I dismissed the warning. After all, what could possibly cause the stability of the financial world to crumble?

Then October 19, 1987, arrived and shocked the stock market and me! Between Tuesday, October 13, and Monday, October 19, the Dow Jones Industrial Average declined by almost one-third—equivalent to a $1 trillion loss in the value of United States stocks. On the day we were able to liquidate our investment, the price was *exactly* what the dream had predicted. We lost tons of money. Discussing the dream's financial impact was off the table, especially since it was my dream and my responsibility to take action.

When I had time to reflect on our financial loss, I was shocked. I wondered how I could have responded differently. There were no indicators other than the dream. Possibly, we could have tried to liquidate the stock and swallow the substantial penalties, but I lacked the courage to stand up for the dream's message. In turn, I had to pay the consequences.

As if this were not enough, I had another powerful dream in December 1987:

I can hear my mother sobbing for her mother, Rosana. Grandma has just died.

The dream jolted me awake. Six months earlier, Grandma had been featured on the CNN Network for her nontraditional work with *remedios*, a tradition of using native herbs for medicinal remedies. In the interview she said in Spanish, "It's important that the knowledge of remedies be passed down through the generations. It has made me more independent with my health care and in control of my health problems."

I remembered years earlier when I was struck with Bell's Palsy. Grandma mailed a *remedio*, rose salve, to rub on my face. Even though the remedy did not regenerate my facial nerve, Grandma's loving wisdom helped me endure an extremely difficult time.

Several weeks later I had an auditory dream:

I hear a gust of wind followed by my mother wailing in grief.

I woke up in a panic. Recently, Grandma had been hospitalized. Mom reassured me, "Don't worry. The doctor said Grandma will be home for Christmas."

After the dream, I was concerned. Time was of the essence. I needed to decide whether to plan a trip to Colorado. In order to make a decision, I spent more time with the dream: *I heard the gusts of wind and Mom sobbing.*

It was painful to hear Mom in such anguish. I realized that, if Grandma was to die, I had to support Mom through this ordeal. It was another way of being Mom's little helper. Even though I had left home over twenty years ago, I was not going to abandon Mom now. After I shared the dream with

Mark, we discussed it and decided to spend Christmas in the Rocky Mountains. I quickly purchased airline tickets since the Christmas season was rapidly approaching. For months Marissa had been preparing for her First Communion at Saint Anthony's Church, but thankfully, our priest gave Marissa permission to receive this sacrament—which was scheduled for Christmas Eve Mass—in Colorado.

When we landed at the rural airport and I walked down the plane's metal stairs, I shivered in the frigid air. Just like in my dream, the wind howled and stirred a turmoil of doubts and questions: *Why were these images coming to me? Was it normal to dream like this? If my family knew, would I be labeled a* bruja, *a witch?*

My intuitive thoughts countered: *Dreams aren't meant to be logical; they have their own reasoning. What is most important is to fully experience the dream and let the experience unfold its meaning.* This response reassured me.

After we settled in Mom and Dad's house, I visited Grandma in the hospital. Suddenly, I heard an authoritative voice emanating from her petite body, which was wrapped in white linen.

"*Tierra*," she demanded.

An aunt responded by gathering the coarse, brown soil that she found outside the hospital. She rubbed it on the bottom of Grandma's feet. Even though Grandma was unresponsive,

I knew that she was a woman of the earth who yearned to touch the brown gritty matter that gave her life sustenance. Just like saying good-bye to her children, Grandma needed to say farewell to the land that had fed her family with a large garden of corn, beans, potatoes, and peas. Nature had given her medicinal herbs that she used to heal others and herself. Rarely had she visited a doctor in her eighty-seven years of life.

One of the last times I saw Grandma, she was in a deep sleep. Overwhelmed by my love and respect for her, I was drawn to kiss her—not once, but several times. I bowed down and kissed her wrinkled forehead that held such deep wisdom. I kissed her soft cheeks of kindness, and I kissed her nose that pointed to the path of healing.

She perked up and said, "*Quien esta besandome?*"

"Grandma, it's me, Cindy, who's kissing you."

She smiled sweetly, and then sleep reached for her again.

It was a minus-thirty-degree Christmas Eve when we attended midnight Mass. In the darkness we drove to church and saw hundreds of *luminarias*, brown bags that hold sand and a lit candle, lining the snowy highway with a magic glow.

In the church, Mark, Andrea, Marissa, and I sat in the front pew while the honorees—Mary, Joseph, and the infant Jesus—rested in the nativity scene. Hundreds of parishioners and their holiday guests filled the church. Red poinsettias decorated the white marble altar, flanked by fifteen-foot

Christmas trees decorated with red, blue, and white bulbs set aglow. The choir sang *Silent Night, Holy Night*. The soft melodies rocked Marissa to sleep. When Communion approached, I nudged her awake. The priest motioned Marissa to the altar. For a moment, everything was silent. No music, no praying, no children crying, just stillness. Marissa looked up at the blue Christmas lights hanging from the ceiling and walked to the altar.

"This is the body of Christ," the priest said.

She leaned toward the priest and said, "Amen."

She returned to the pew and knelt.

Later, Marissa said, "Mommy, I felt so special. I was the only one receiving communion."

One night a few years earlier, Marissa had encountered Christ after I tucked her into bed. As I was washing my face over the sink, she walked into the bathroom.

"Someone turned off the lights in heaven."

"What do you mean?" I tried to hide my shock.

"Jesus was walking towards me when all of a sudden he disappeared. Then everything went black."

"Ohhh."

Marissa turned around and, with a veil of concern, walked back to her bedroom.

On this Christmas Eve as Marissa was absorbing the body of Christ, Grandma Rosana was reaching her heavenly destination.

We returned from church exhausted and went to bed. An hour later, my sister shook me awake. "Grandma has died."

I jumped out of bed. Mom quickly dressed, too, and I drove her to the hospital. I was her shadow as we rushed through the corridor. Mom opened the door to Grandma's room. She saw Grandma's body, and crumpled on top of it while she wailed. I stood quietly next to Mom as she told her mother, "*Mamacita, te quiero mucho.*" She spoke as if Grandma were listening to her words of love.

Grandma's physical presence was gone, but I knew that she had shared the same essence of the wise Feminine that over a year ago had embraced me in Einsiedeln. Grandma was a Crone who had gathered flowers of wisdom as she walked on the hot coals of life. Grandma often said:

"Life is like a well—as one bucket empties, the other fills."

"Trust in God."

"Never be afraid to die."

"Material things aren't important."

My dreams created the opportunity for this once-in-a-life-time experience when I was able to say good-bye to this honorable woman who spoke only Spanish. I had struggled to understand our ancestral language, but I was fluent in her world of healing and compassion. She was my godmother, a woman who held me as an infant while I was blessed on the crown of my head and baptized into the Catholic Church. And she taught me to respect the health-giving powers of the natural world.

Between the combination of Grandma's death and our financial loss, I was convinced that working with dreams was as natural as breathing fresh air. Through my own experiences and in working with my clients' dreams, I learned that most auditory dreams can be taken literally. Typically, the unconscious communicates through symbols. But in the auditory dream when I heard Mom crying and the wind howling, the unconscious spoke directly, needing little interpretation.

After these two incidents, every part of my being— emotional, intellectual, and spiritual—made the commitment to have a relationship with my dreams. As if I had extended my hand to the unconscious, it reached for mine and gave me a gift in a conceptual framework.

Months later, in another dream I saw the following words:

On paper, draw a line in the middle of the page from top to bottom, similar to pages in a stenographer's notebook. On the left side of the line, write the dream exactly as it presents itself. After writing the dream, circle (key words) that generate strong responses.

Then on the right side of the line, free-associate to the words that are circled. Write the words, images or memories that emerge.

The discipline of writing the dream in a methodical manner was complemented by intuitively free-associating with the symbols. From left to right was a continuum from unconsciousness to consciousness. Using it like a worksheet, the dream suggested these steps: write the dream, circle key words that hold a lot of energy, and free-associate with the circled words. On the left-hand side of the paper, the unconscious generated dream symbols. I wrote associations, memories, or feelings on the right hand side of the line that corresponded to these symbols. This exercise initiated an awareness that was not present before the dream. I reflected on the words written on the right-hand side to help bring into awareness an insight about a particular issue or a personal dynamic. *[In this book circled key words are indicated with parentheses.]*

After working on a dream, I asked myself: *How can I integrate this awareness into my everyday life? Has the dream given me a different perspective about a situation or an insight on a characteristic that I need to work on?* I continued working on the dream until I had an inner "Aha" moment when something clicked—an insight from the unconscious flashed into consciousness or into my awareness.

The following key guideline was imperative in working with my dreams: as soon as possible, I wrote the dream in a journal *exactly* as it presented itself, no matter if it was in the middle of the night or first thing in the morning. My first dream journal was a stenographer's notebook, because a line was already printed down the middle of the page like in my dream.

I kept this journal on my nightstand so that I could easily grab it without gambling that I might forget the dream. Oftentimes, I swore I would never forget such a dream, so why should I bother writing it down? But if I forgot to write it, more often than not, within seconds, any fragment of the dream was gone. A client once said that she had forgotten to write her dream. She had felt it slipping back into the unconscious. She had tried to reel it back, but it had vanished.

From a logical perspective, my dreams seemed silly and irrational. Sometimes, I thought: *That crazy dream. I'm too embarrassed to talk to anyone about it. They'll think I'm whacko*. But from an intuitive perspective, my dreams offered a process of listening to my emotions, memories, and bodily reactions, which served as a bridge to the Feminine. Working with dreams was like learning a foreign language; the more I practiced, the more fluent I became. Also, dreams always kept my ego in check. Working with the Feminine required that I continuously surrender to the Divine.

In spite of clients and friends telling me that they never dream, research shows that everyone dreams, but drugs, daily stress and lack of sleep interfere with remembering them. Dreams have existed for eons. The Bible contains one hundred dreams—images that led the prophets to the Promised Land. Christianity was saved when Joseph listened to an angel in his dream.

"Get up," the angel said. "Take the child and his mother to escape to Egypt. Stay there until I tell you, for Herod is going to search for the child to kill him." So Joseph took Jesus and Mary during the night to Egypt and stayed there until Herod died.

Many times, the actual words in a dream contain a story. Jungian analyst, Russell A. Lockhart, cautioned in the book, *Soul and Money,* that a definition of a word is only its shell that covers the word's soul. He accuses people of being word abusers, because the genesis of the word is overlooked. Words contained stories of history, places, and people. If a particular word in a dream captured my attention, I looked it up in a dictionary. I became a detective and searched for its definition, its history, and its root. I read the story of the word until it came alive. I did the same with the words in my own dreams.

Sometimes, at breakfast, Marissa and Andrea often talked about their dreams. Andrea was excited.

"Mommy, my Little Ponies were in my dream last night."

"Really, how exciting. What were they doing?"

"They were running all around me. I wanted to jump on them, but I couldn't catch them. I'm too small."

"You love those ponies, don't you?"

"Yeaaa."

I avoided analyzing Andrea's dream. Mostly, I tried to acknowledge her emotions. By sharing their dreams, the girls were establishing a tradition of valuing their dream life and making it conscious by talking about their reactions.

All dream imagery is referred to as symbols. One client, Eileen, who was thirty-five years old, referred to symbols as "those dream people." Those people were bringing information to Eileen, like building blocks for her psychological development. One of the symbols was the Torah. Eileen, who was Protestant, was drawn to Judaism. She yearned to learn Hebrew, participate in Sabbath rituals, and learn how to bake challah.

"Are your parents or any relatives Jewish?" I asked.

"I've asked my Mom and Dad, and they've said no."

"Well, there's a part of you that yearns for Judaism whether you're Jewish or not."

After several months in therapy, Eileen walked into my office and appeared to be eager to tell me something. She sat down.

"They finally told me the truth."

I leaned toward her. "What truth are you talking about?"

"My parents are Jewish."

Silence. We both sat in the purity of her truth.

In order to make her whole and complete, Eileen's dream symbols had awakened her family history and deepened her spiritual roots while enriching her life. She incorporated the dream's wisdom into her daily life by learning Hebrew and fasting during Sabbath.

And so not only was I able to integrate dreams into my own life, I also saw them deeply inform and guide others to the truth of their lives, such as the sound of my mother sobbing, Marissa's experience of Jesus, Andrea's Little Ponies, and Eileen's intuition of her family's history. As an expression of Eileen's appreciation of our dreamwork, she painted a scene of Haystack Rock at Cannon Beach, in the brilliance of a setting sun, as a gift for me.

Chapter Eight

DIFFICULTY BREATHES RENEWAL

Mark spotted a beautiful 320-acre farm that was for sale when we visited Colorado for Grandma's funeral. Months earlier, Mark's company had been acquired by a business headquartered in Boston. This acquisition had left us financially independent, and we could live anywhere. The Oregon coast was my first choice since we owned a beach house there. The Rocky Mountains did not even make my short list.

At dinner, Mark and I sat at the kitchen table discussing buying the farm. He was so excited.

"The farm house has potential. We can renovate it. It's such a beautiful farm with the old-fashioned red barn. The owner is going into foreclosure, so we can't beat the price."

"Would you like more coffee?" I asked, so I could think about my argument.

"No, I've had enough."

"You know," I began, hoping to discourage him, "You'd

have to find someone to help you farm. Three hundred twenty acres is a lot of land."

"Yeah, I'm sure we can find help. And it'll be a good place for Andrea and Marissa."

I persisted "I never thought I'd return to the Valley. It was a great place to grow up, but I'm not sure I want to live there again."

He did not hear me. "Oh, I just remembered a dream that I had last night. I'm looking into an old barn similar to the one I saw in Colorado. It was filled with grain."

A dream. I could not ignore it. "Was there anything else?"

He described his dream of bountiful sustenance that comes from the land, and I relented. "Well, maybe, we can get someone in the family to help us."

Fortunately, my dreams pointed in the same direction. The dream worksheet helped to analyze the following dreams:

November 15, 1987

I'm in (Colorado) on my parents' farm. I am standing next to a metal gate by the maroon barn petting, a (buffalo) with a thick, shaggy head.	Home, where I grew up, Western US

In the second dream:

November 22, 1987

I'm sitting on a plane destined for a vacation in Spain. I'm peering through a window, and to my surprise, instead of landing in Madrid, the pilot (lands on a highway)	Shock, change in plans
that runs next to my parents' house. I look out the window and see my father standing in an alfalfa field	Colorado
hugging a (black cow).	Symbol of the Feminine

When I worked with these dreams, buffalo, black cow, Colorado, and shock emerged. I was aware that whenever an animal appeared in my dreams, I was given the opportunity to use this animal's energy. First, I had to free-associate to the animal. If the animal was totally foreign to me, I researched the animal in my favorite book, Ted Andrews's *Animal Speak:*

The Spiritual & Magical Powers of Creatures Great & Small.
I asked myself, *What does this animal want to teach me? How can I use this animal's essence in my life? Even when their spirit terrifies me, how can I befriend it?*

When I free-associated to the buffalo, I thought of the West, where at one time, millions of buffalos roamed the prairie. When I studied the buffalo, I read that it was known for its bulky upper body. Head first, the buffalo marches into a storm rather than running away from it. Perhaps I needed to walk into the turbulence of my life rather than avoiding it, like this possible move to Colorado. Maybe the buffalo was showing me how to lower my head and push forward.

The cow is often associated with the Feminine, the archetype that nurtures. With Daddy hugging its head, I was reminded that I needed to befriend this instinct to nurture. Perhaps my work with the Feminine needed to continue in Colorado.

The dream shocked me, because I was planning a trip to Spain. But the dream suggested that Colorado was my destination.

In spite of the minus-thirty-five-degree weather we had tolerated during Grandma's funeral, Mark was drawn to live at this particular farm. Even with the guidance of these dreams, I had trepidation, but we listed our house on the market.

My friends and colleagues challenged our decision about the move.

"Why would you want to change your lifestyle and profession?"

"What makes you want to live in an isolated valley in Colorado?"

"Where are you going to find a good caffe latte? You have to really think about this one and not be too rash."

My colleagues felt so sorry for me that they gave me an espresso machine as a going away present. My friends' questions reflected my own doubts. Living in Seattle was like living in the belly of the ocean. Salmon, clams, scallops, and oysters thrived in the waters of Puget Sound. The snow-capped peaks of Mount Rainer and Mount Baker looked like vanilla ice cream sundaes. The Olympic range gave the illusion of mountains rising from the Pacific Ocean. Like the lush vegetation and colorful landscape, the Emerald City had brought new life in the form of Andrea and Marissa. Mark had cofounded his computer company here, and I had launched my private practice.

As I was transitioning from Puget Sound toward the Rocky Mountains, I was finding it difficult to say farewell to this beautiful city.

Mark drove to Colorado for the closing on the farm and to oversee the remodeling of the house. Andrea, Marissa, and

I were left behind so the girls could continue attending school, and I could close my client load and prepare for the move. I suddenly realized that I had a problem. How was I going to take the icon of the Black Madonna to Colorado? Mark had already left. Shipping her was out of the question; if the painting was lost, I could never replace it. A simple, but expensive solution was to buy the icon an airline ticket and have it sit next to me. What a great idea! I telephoned our travel agent.

"May I help you?"

"Yes, we're moving to Colorado. And I need to make a reservation for the Black Madonna—one way."

"The what?"

"She is a valuable icon, and I don't want her in baggage."

"How large is this icon?"

"She's about 20 inches by 31 inches."

"Put her in a box, and we'll place her next to you."

I thought the problem was resolved until we boarded the plane. The box barely fit in the seat. This trip was prior to the 9/11 catastrophe in 2001. Post-9/11 airport security would have required that such a large box be checked as baggage.

"What's in the box?" a passenger who sat across the aisle whispered.

"It's an icon of the Black Madonna."

"Oh." She looked away with a perplexed look.

The flight attendant walked down the aisle and screamed, "That box absolutely cannot stay in that seat!"

"But that box has a ticket to sit in that seat," I said. I put my arms around the box as if it were my child.

"Absolutely not! You cannot leave it there! I'm placing this package in the carry-on closet. Contact your travel agent for a refund."

I had no choice but to let go of the Madonna and give her to the flight attendant. All I cared about was placing the Madonna in a secured area.

Hours later, the attendant announced, "In twenty minutes we will be descending to Denver's Stapleton Airport." As the flight attendant walked past me, she whispered, "I placed your box in first class."

Perfect spot for the Madonna, I thought.

As I glanced at Marissa sitting in her seat (Andrea had flown earlier with my father, Tiofilo), I tried to muster up the same excitement I once felt as an enthusiastic adolescent who gathered wood in the San Juan Mountains. I remembered the buffalo that was giving me determination and encouraging me to lower my head into the turbulence of change.

Marissa, the icon of the Black Madonna, and I connected with a commuter flight—without any flight attendant on board to question my box—to the closest airport to the farm. As we flew over the Rocky Mountains, I looked down at the largest Alpine valley in the world rising to 8,000 feet above sea level. Over two centuries ago, southern Colorado was the northern tip of the Viceroyalty of New Spain, often referred to as the New Frontier—land that still offered new adventures and opportunities for the Black Madonna and me.

Chapter Nine

SPIRITUAL TRANSFORMATION

Spring in Seattle looked like a Monet masterpiece with sunny daffodils and tulips in rainbow colors next to rhododendrons with pearly-white blossoms. Leafy azaleas showing off their maroon-pink flowers bowed in splendor while silent rain rested on their soft petals. I packed away this memory of Seattle's brilliant springtime when I left the Pacific Northwest.

My latent sadness appeared when Mark forgot to pick up Marissa and me at the airport. I found a telephone and called him. "Hi! Marissa and I are waiting for you at the airport."

"Oh, I forgot that you were coming today. I'll be right there."

He did not apologize. I looked at Marissa and shrugged my shoulders. "Daddy will be here soon." I thought, *How could he have forgotten that we were coming? Is this some kind of omen?*

After we waited thirty minutes, Mark drove up in his

truck. We reluctantly hugged and kissed, and he threw our luggage in the bed of the pickup.

Mark drove us to the farm where the land looked like dry leather. What I found in the San Luis Valley was in stark contrast to the Pacific Northwest. It was one thing to visit my family and know I would be returning to Seattle, but it was another matter to know I would be permanently living here. I was unsure this was what I wanted at age thirty-five, especially after Mark's lack of consideration.

The dirt road was lined with centuries-old cottonwood trees encrusted with thick bark that looked like deep ravines, where horses sought cool shade on hot afternoons. Wooden corrals circled a faded red barn. This farm was once a well-known horse ranch that bred noble Percheron that weighed as much as 1,850 pounds. These great horses were used for the mines in Leadville, Colorado, that required a class of horses that could tolerate the high altitude, steep inclines, and the deepest snow. The guesthouse, where we would be living until the main house was renovated, was at the end of the road. I spent the following weeks unpacking and getting acquainted with this land.

I was suddenly reminded of the terrible weather. I had forgotten about the unbearable spring winds that blew twenty-four hours a day and sapped all my motivation. Our visits home had mostly been in the summer or for Christmas.

Marissa, Andrea, and I were going to visit Grandma Priscilla and Grandpa Tiofilo, who lived a few miles away. I opened the front door and caught it before it was slammed against the wall.

"Girls, hold on to me."

We walked out and closed the door. The wind slapped me around with dust particles flying into my eyes and scratching my contacts. "Let's get in the car as fast as we can."

I opened the back door, and the girls jumped in. I plopped into the driver's seat with my wild hair now full of dirt. I looked like I had just jumped out of bed. My eyes were tearing, and it felt like needles were piercing them. I looked in the rearview mirror at Marissa and Andrea who were shaking the dust out of their hair.

"Are you girls okay?"

"Yeah," they said in unison. They looked bewildered about this new farm life.

What was meant to be "spring" slowly melded into summer, which brought swarms of mosquitoes that could have carried away the orphan lambs that were affectionately called *pencos*. Marissa and Andrea ran into the kitchen with the greenish-glass pop bottles and rubber nipples. "Mom, hurry and fill the bottles with milk. The *pencos* are hungry."

"Andrea, wait a second. Their milk can't be too hot or too cold. They like it lukewarm."

I filled the bottles with milk and fastened the rubber nipples. The girls wrapped their arms around the bottles and left for the barn.

Minutes later Marissa and Andrea walked into the kitchen with the empty bottles and with their carefully chosen tops and shorts splattered with milk. The hungry *pencos* had sucked so hard that they had yanked the nipples off the bottles and sprayed milk everywhere. Every time they tried to feed the lambs, the scenario was the same.

One day, Andrea, with all her enthusiasm and tenderness, climbed into the matchstick corral to pet and hug the fuzzy lambs only to encounter the mother ewe. The sheep stomped her hoof twice as a warning, then lowered her head and rammed it into Andrea's stomach. Andrea learned that day to never get between a mother and her baby.

In the midst of all the activities on the farm, Mark was busy with chores and remodeling our home. His work continued, but in a different form.

At eighteen years old, I had left the San Luis Valley for college. I only returned to the Valley for breaks, and once married, we returned for family vacations. I had always wondered what it would be like to live closer to my family, and now I was finding out. Birthdays, anniversaries, baptisms, and weddings were regularly celebrated with lots of food and music.

Andrea and Marissa spent lots of time playing with their cousins, too. Sometimes they asked Marissa, "Where do you live?"

"Seattle."

I shared Marissa's longing for city life, conversations with close friends, interactions with neighbors, discussions about psychological dynamics with colleagues, and meals of scrumptious fresh salmon sprinkled with dill and butter-dipped crab.

There was nothing fresh and buttery about rural life with its slower pace. I found its simplicity unbearable. The busy treadmill pace that I was accustomed to was reduced to a crawl. I was used to running like the horses that once galloped on this ranch. Racing to appointments with clients, driving Marissa and Andrea to their swimming classes, and rushing home to cook dinner were no longer necessary. The extra time that I had yearned for in Seattle was now in abundance, and somehow I was lost.

I was unsure what direction my life was going to take. Working was not necessary since selling the computer company met our financial needs. I was satisfied in my profession of psychotherapy, but it was demanding and required total commitment and dedication to my clients' processes. I decided to allow myself as much time as I needed to consider all my options.

Consequently, I was left without the persona of a professional, the wife of a CEO, and a colleague. I felt naked without these titles and roles. For a bit, I thought I had misinterpreted my dreams and my intuition that had partly led us to Colorado. Surely, making the right choices would guarantee an easy transition. Wrong. The symbols in my dreams brought inspiration and energy for these changes, but it was up to me to make the necessary adjustments.

Shopping could have been a distraction for me, but shopping malls and Nordstrom's "personal shoppers" were nowhere. The closest movie theatre was twenty miles away. When the moving company delivered our furniture and the driver turned the long green truck to leave, I wanted to step in front of him and shout, "Please take me with you. I don't care where you're going as long as it's away from here!"

I reduced traveling outside the Valley to a minimum, because I could not trust myself to return.

Friends who lived in the city asked with excitement, "How does it feel to move to the country? I've always imagined how fun it would be to live on a farm."

I sighed and said, "It's been difficult. It's not as romantic and thrilling as you might think."

My empty life felt intolerable. The words of Saint John

of the Cross helped me to understand the importance of this hollowness:

> To reach satisfaction in all
>
> desire satisfaction in nothing.
>
> To come to possess all
>
> desire the possession of nothing.
>
> To arrive at being all
>
> desire to be nothing.
>
> To come to the knowledge of all
>
> desire the knowledge of nothing.

In this "nothingness" I felt like a lonely seed buried in the dark earth covered with snow, yearning for spring's warmth but uncertain about its arrival.

In the meantime, there was always entertainment featuring the antics of the farm animals. One day, I looked out the kitchen window, and to my dismay, I saw the kid goats—with their natural taupe-colored vests and white running socks—playing tag on the hoods of the cars parked next to each other. The miniature goats chased each other back and forth, from one shiny hood to the next, their hooves scratching the paint off the metal. I ran outside and shooed them off the vehicles. They jumped in the air with a click, click of their hooves, then ran to their next adventure.

Oh my God! I mumbled more than once.

I realized that fighting against Nature's instincts, whether it was the howling wind or the kid goats' orneriness, was futile. I learned that appearances and material possessions had no significance on the farm. So what if the vehicles had scratches on them? The lambs and goats could care less. Slowly, I was letting go of my need for perfection. I could wash the cars over and over again, but the next second they would be dirty. As a child growing up on the farm, we were always playing outside and getting muddy. Back then, "perfection" was not in my vocabulary. Slowly, I let go of my need to control Nature, and with this I was allowing my true instincts to emerge.

The Alamosa River that meandered through the northern boundaries of our property became my refuge. I spent hours there meditating and reflecting on the challenges of rural life and the stability I had left behind. Then I started noticing the river's embankment wrapped with purple irises. The water's melody was like an orchestra of violins serenading the fish as they swam under the roots of a tree dug deep in the river—the melody entertained me, too. Sitting on the grass, I relaxed and inhaled the natural beauty surrounding me. When I thought about those rambunctious kid goats, I felt the warmth of a smile. My resistance to this life began to shift.

One day when I was walking home on the dusty road at almost 8,000 feet above sea level, I imagined tiptoeing and touching the billowy clouds. The mist against the ethereal sky enraptured me. I stared into the turquoise sky, waiting in anticipation. Suddenly, I saw the divine guest. Jesus Christ himself was standing on a cloud, dressed in a long saffron-colored robe, with long hair and a beard. He leaned down, grabbed my hand, and kissed my skin. A surge of strength coupled with tenderness flowed through my body. His powerfully sweet love permeated my entire being. He stood up and then pointed to his Sacred Heart. Then he evaporated into the clouds without leaving a single remnant of his flowing robe or his gentle face— just the gift of his sacred love. I was left staring at the clouds. I could barely move. Finally, I walked home, wondering if I had really seen Jesus, or had it been my imagination?

Later, when I discussed my vision with my analyst who lived in Seattle, he advised, "Just *be* with the experience."

After we finished our phone session, I sank into my chair. Jesus's love was too much to absorb at one time. I felt unworthy of His presence and love for me. Why would Christ want to appear to me? I am as ordinary as they come. Maybe a little lost and without a direction, but basically a simple farm girl. Once I was able to quiet this inner chatter, I remained with His all-consuming love—a love of strength and tenderness. I covered my face with my hands until they held a tidal pool of tears.

My experience reminded me of a time when I stood next to the majestic California redwoods. I felt like an ant compared to these trees that had been standing centuries before I was born and would continue to witness the evolution of humankind. I had a glimpse of antiquity.

I wrote about my vision of Jesus:

The gates of heaven are opening.

I know because the clouds tell me so.

The celestial mist funnels across the sky,

announcing the coming guest.

The parade of clouds continues,

trumpeting the excitement of who is to come.

The heavens call me to watch . . . I await.

The sky turns crimson. I see him. I am paralyzed.

It is Jesus, robed in red pointing to his Sacred Heart.

He extends his hand. Mine meets his.

He kisses it with gentleness and strength unknown to me.

It is Gentle Jesus, gentle as a lamb, with his heart burning with flames of love.

This vision challenged my way of thinking and feeling. I struggled to absorb this Christ-love. Up to this point, my life was etched in polarities. A person was either strong or weak; thinking or feeling; masculine or feminine. With this kiss, Jesus melded all opposites into one spiritual being.

Sometimes, I asked myself, *Why are these visions coming to me?* But I knew I had no control over my spiritual instincts, any more than I could control the wind.

On another day, the clouds evoked another vision. I saw a man sitting on a cloud. He had a long white beard and was dressed in a flowing brown robe. He looked stern and authoritative, almost like he was mad about something. In his right hand, he held a silver ring with several skeleton keys. I did not recognize this man, but his seriousness impressed me. Later, I was thumbing through a book on pictures of saints. There he was: Saint Peter.

In retrospect, I believe the mystical images were preparing my psyche and my body as if they were containers that needed to be strengthened to carry new ideas and realizations. My mind and my physicality had to be strong enough to hold this energy and not be overwhelmed or be broken by it. Jesus, pointing to his heart, was a reminder of God's love for me, an infinite source of strength and courage for whatever lay ahead. If Saint Peter held the keys to heaven, I better be as serious about how I lived my life as he was about unlocking the door to eternity.

And I was confident that this intuitive spiritual world of images and visions would show me the way.

If someone had asked me, "Where were you when the 'big one' happened?" as if the event were a ten-point-zero earthquake, I could say that I was walking down the lane to the mailbox. Actually, I have no idea what I was doing. The activity or the location faded in the background when compared to what was in the forefront. Several days later, out of nowhere, in my inner eye I saw an image of Jesus kneeling in prayer in the Garden of Gethsemane before his crucifixion.

I was familiar with this image. When I lived in Seattle, my crown chakra had opened with amazing intensity that felt like bees swarming through my hair. I had to jump in a bathtub full of water to ground this energy. When I emerged from the bath water, I saw this same image of Christ praying in the Garden of Gethsemane. Right then, I had no idea that this was the beginning of a sequence of events that would be pivotal in my spiritual development.

In the Valley, after several weeks of seeing Jesus praying, in my inner eye the image changed; instead of Jesus hanging on the cross, in horror and disbelief, I saw myself nailed to wood, a cross that was next to the altar in the church that I attended. I was wearing my favorite blue pants with a white top, so there was no mistake that it was I nailed to the cross. I was left weak and nauseous. I mumbled, "How can this be?" It took time to process this experience.

In the following days, anything made me cry. It felt like I would shatter into a million pieces if someone accidentally bumped into me. This sensation of brokenness made me feel fragile and vulnerable, naked without any clothes. And I was filled with melancholy as if I had lost my dearest friend. All I could do was continue to tolerate these difficult feelings. The key was staying present with my emotions and avoiding activities that would have taken me away from this experience.

Later, I gained understanding by reflecting on my crucifixion. My ego, my dearest friend and vital to my psyche, had to surrender to the Divine, no matter how painful it was. This step was essential in my spiritual transformation, because my ego was not in control of my spirituality. When the ego believes it is in control of this archetypal energy, this phenomenon is referred to as "possessed by an archetype," which can be extremely dangerous, teetering on an implosion. My ego was a partner with this archetypal energy. It certainly was not in charge of it.

Indeed, I had lost an old belief system that had shaped me for the last thirty-five years. As an American, individualism had molded my behavior and philosophy. I was proud to repeat adages like:

"I'm the architect of my future."

"I'm in charge of my destiny."

"I'm in control and can accomplish anything that *I* want."

I had been nailed to the cross, and my ego was no longer dictating my future. I was no longer in the driver seat—in fact, the keys had been snatched away from me. Now, I was only the passenger. Ever so slowly, as the days progressed, the sensation of brokenness subsided.

I only revealed this experience to one or two of my trusted friends. I was afraid that others might think I was sacrilegious. Everyone knew that only Jesus was supposed to be on the cross. But I was still searching for someone with authority to approve my spiritual experiences and say that I was still a devout Catholic. I was especially close to our parish priest. I wanted to share this experience with him, but I remembered his reaction when I shared my experience with the Black Madonna while I was studying in Switzerland. He did not use either the word delirious or sacrilegious; actually he hardly said a word. I was afraid to think what was going on his mind, and I did not ask. That was the last day that I ever sought any affirmation about my spirituality from the Catholic Church. No one could have given me the value of authority that I needed to give myself. Mass and my spiritual practices complemented each other. The sacraments, the Mass, the stained glass windows of the saints and their inspiring lives, and the music all fed my spirituality. My visions and their gifts from the Divine stood in their own integrity. Certainly, sharing my "crucifixion" experience with the parish priest was not necessary.

In a conversation, on another topic, with a close friend who was also a wise bishop, he said, "Never let anyone stand between you and your God." Amen.

Out of nowhere, my cousin Arnold telephoned me. He was researching our maternal family genealogy on the Quintana side. I never knew what his next discovery was going to be.

"Hi *prima*, how are you doing?"

Before I could respond he continued. "Have you heard about this book that was written by two professors: one teaches at the University of California in Santa Barbara, and the other one teaches at Whitman College in Washington state?"

"Can't say I have."

"The book is about Miguel Quintana, our tenth-generation grandfather. We should be able to buy it soon."

And that was my introduction to Francisco A. Lomelí and Clark A. Colahan's book, *Defying the Inquisition in Colonial New Mexico: Miguel de Quintana's Life and Writings*. Miguel de Quintana was a mystic who wrote about his relationship with God during a dangerous period in church history. The Spanish Inquisition was burning people at the stake for their nonconformity to Spain and to the Catholic Church.

In the year 1695, at the age of sixteen, Miguel, his wife,

and in-laws left Mexico City with a caravan of colonists accompanying Don Diego de Vargas Zapata Luján Ponce de León to reconquer the kingdom of northern Mexico. I can only imagine the courage and tenacity Miguel and his family needed to venture into the New Frontier after living a comfortable life in Mexico City. The caravan settled on their allotted land grant north of Santa Fe into a political center called *La Villa Nueva de Santa Cruz de la Cañada* de Españoles Mexicanos del Rey Nuestro Señor *Carlos Segundo* (The New Villa of Santa Cruz of the Cañada of Mexican Spaniards under the King, our Lord, Charles II), also known as Santa Cruz.

Miguel was a literate man, which elevated him to a central figure in the community. He was the town scribe and signed banns of marriage (a required formal announcement about the intent to marry) and penned legal documents. The colonists traveled El Camino Real to reach new opportunities, but unimaginable poverty also awaited them. With Miguel's growing family of ten children and faced with crop failure, they were "obliged to eat dog, horse, and mule meat; toasted skins; & foul-smelling weeds and grasses," according to Lomelí and Colahan.

Miguel composed personal prayers for weddings and eulogies, in addition to original plays and mystical writings. The Spanish Inquisition murdered people who had individual relationships with God outside the church. Among the requirements for the colonists leaving Mexico City was to be "of good

Christian character" or, more appropriately, good Christian character according to the Spanish Inquisition. When Miguel told the parish priests about his mystical writings, they reported him to the Spanish Inquisition in Mexico City, which prompted an investigation into his writings. Miguel was emotionally shattered. His personal tenacity of faith that had given him strength and conviction to explore and settle in the New Frontier was now his burden and possibly his demise.

In Miguel's writings, the Mother of God spoke to him during the investigation. Below are Miguel's words written in his Spanish language and translated into English, according to Lomelí and Colahan:

> *Soy la Madre de la esperanza,*
>   I am the Mother of hope,
> *soy llave y puerta del cielo,*
>   I am the key and door of heaven,
> *soy refugio donde hallan*
>   I am the refuge
> *los afligidos Consuelo*
>   where the afflicted find solace.
>
> *Eso la Iglesia lo canta*
>   That is what the Church sings
> *con himnos y salmos y versos.*
>   in hymns and psalms and verses.
> *Mira, Miguel, si habra quien,*
>   Do you think, Miguel,
> *óbice ponga a tus versos.*
>   anyone will find fault with your poems?

Guardalos, Miguel, y aguarda
    Keep them, Miguel, and wait
muy grande alivio y Consuelo
    for a very great relief and consolation,
que en unos y en otros gozas
    for in every last one
auxilios muy verdaderos.
    you find a very true help.

These words encouraged Miguel during the investigation of his alleged heresy. In 1737, around the age of sixty, he was exonerated by the court. Around that time his creative writings stopped or became clandestine. His pardoning may have resulted from a declaration that he was delusional or had a "damaged imagination." Miguel seemed to yield to their decision. Ironically, in the court's attempt to silence Miguel and destroy his writings, they accomplished the opposite. His writings were required to be preserved in the Spanish Inquisition Archives in Mexico City where they exist to this day. During the Spanish Inquisition, thousands of people—the exact number will never be known—were burned at the stake, and thousands of books were destroyed. Grandpa Miguel's writings were not only spared; but were preserved.

Grandpa Miguel died a natural death on April 9, 1748. One hundred years later, the Mexican-American War started and subsequently ended with the signing of the Treaty of Guadalupe Hidalgo. This treaty gave the United States parts of New Mexico, as well as parts of Colorado, Arizona, Utah, and Nevada for $15 million. The United States Constitution provided its new citizens with the First Amendment that guaranteed freedom of (and from) religion.

Lomelí and Colahan described Miguel's challenges as "issues of individual conscience versus social conformity, freedom of speech versus censorship, personal mysticism versus dogma, and, finally, the embedded values of hegemony of a Spanish colony versus the emergent values of enlightened humanism in a nascent community." Cousin Arnold and I sponsored a book signing for authors Lomelí and Colahan in Santa Cruz, New Mexico. When I met Professor Lomelí, he signed his book, "You can't imagine what a pleasure it is to reconnect with Quintana descendants. *Gracia, gracia.*" he wrote.

Two and one-half centuries had passed between Grandpa Miguel's life and mine. What did censorship look like in my life that was now nurturing a mystical emergence? Was it the parish priest whose silence I interpreted as negating my mystical experience? Maybe it was a friend who asked, "Why didn't I have the encounter with Black Madonna instead of you?" I almost apologized to her because of my need for acceptance.

Today, I would respond to my friend, "The Black Madonna is an intrinsic aspect of your psyche, as well as an aspect of every man and woman, regardless of their religious association.

The Black Madonna waits in prayer and in meditation for an endearing relationship with you."

Another face of dominance was my fear of rejection by the Catholic Church. Because of this pressure, I might have ignored or tried to negate these mystical experiences. On the other hand, the support that I received from my analyst and my friends helped me to acknowledge and integrate these spiritual visions.

The Mother of God said to Miguel, "You find a very true help." Miguel's relationship with God helped him to overcome challenges of food shortages, settling in a hostile environment, plagues, and to add insult to injury, the Spanish Inquisition. The Mother of God empowered Miguel through his writings to continue on his path in spite of the Inquisition.

In many ways, the psyche that exists in the twenty-first century is no different than the one that lived in the seventeenth century. I needed divine intercession in my new life in the Valley. True help was within me, no matter where I existed. My dreams inspired me and made me strong and courageous in order to trust in the knowledge of the Spirit. I thought my wealth was in dollars and cents, but my true value was in my relationship with God. I wondered where this New Frontier of the soul would take me.

Jungian analyst Helen M. Luke offered a hint in her book, *Woman, Earth, and Spirit: The Feminine in Symbol and Myth*:

If we can rediscover in ourselves the hidden beauty of this receptive devotion; if we can learn how to be still without inaction, how to "further life" without willed purpose, how to serve without demanding prestige, and how to nourish without domination: then we shall be women again out of whose earth the light may shine.

Chapter Ten

THE SACRIFICE OF PARTING

In July 1988, four months after we arrived in the Valley, we started moving our furniture and other belongings into our remodeled house, which was just across the dirt road from the guest house where we had been staying. Our moving boxes contained not only our personal belongings, but unresolved issues in our marriage that I had packed away while living in Seattle.

Mark and I had cleared many hurdles in our fourteen-year marriage. We had sacrificed intimacy and time together in order to attain a successful computer business and a psychotherapeutic practice. Unfortunately, we had spent more time apart than together. The demanding corporate world had left little time to share our frustrations and feelings.

There were a number of conflicts that arose again and again. Mark's mood swings were unpredictable. I took a lot of pride in cooking delicious, sometimes gourmet, meals. When we all sat around the dining room table to eat, within five minutes Mark had finished his meal. I wondered how he could appreciate the saffron spice or the marinated sirloin when he inhaled his food.

I asked in irritation, "Why do you eat so fast? I shouldn't bother cooking this food. By the time I sit down, you're already finished eating."

With a hint of sarcasm he replied, "At the Air Force Academy, we had to eat fast."

That was twenty years ago, I thought.

Another issue was that Mark just could not let go of world events. One time, I used a knife to open a package, and it slipped out of my fingers and stabbed my foot. Luckily, when I pulled out the knife, I avoided cutting any arteries. Unfortunately, the wound became infected and required surgery. At the time, there was an uprising in Central America. While I was lying in the hospital bed in extreme pain, Mark started screaming about the left-wing politics there.

I wanted to say, "I'm fed up with world politics. I'm in terrible pain. I'm waiting to be wheeled into surgery, and all you can talk about is politics. I'm scared to death of this surgery!" But again, I suppressed my frustrations. After I came out of recovery, he had calmed down, and I was glad he was there.

I realized that Mark's absence when he traveled and worked fourteen-hour days had served a purpose. It had helped me to tolerate his unreasonable behavior. How could he harass me if he was traveling hundreds of miles away? I was no longer on edge waiting to see what was irritating him.

Now, we were in the Valley, trying to move into our new home. As I started carrying boxes into the house, in my inner eye, I saw a black bull that was refusing to cross the front door's threshold. I placed my back against its butt and tried to shove its body through the door. The bull would not budge.

I was aware that when an animal appeared in my dreams or in a vision, in some way my life needed the essence and the energy of this animal. The image of the bull had appeared to me several times earlier. The bull and the Black Madonna seemed an unlikely partnership. But the receptive Feminine that was a vessel for new ideas and novel projects needed the Masculine's assertiveness to take these new ideas and projects into the world.

Symbols, in dreams and in visions, have real energy that is felt throughout the physical body. The bull, as a symbol, carried sexual energy that needed to be released in a creative way. I tried to express this energy in my sexual relationship with Mark, but I sensed his uneasiness about my new behavior. So, I reverted back to my old timid ways. However, I soon realized that I needed an environment that encouraged *my* ideas, *my* perceptions, and *my* new behavior.

I asked myself, *What were some of the other reasons why I didn't want to step foot into this* large *remodeled home?* My only request to Mark was that I wanted a *smaller* house than what we had owned in Seattle. I was always challenged by cleaning the house. Finally, I had to hire a cleaning person to help me. I did fine growing up in a small house where four of us slept in the same room. I thought a large home was a waste of space and a waste of utilities. Soon I realized that downsizing the house reflected my need for closeness. As it turned out, this home was double the square footage of our home in Seattle.

When we first moved to the Valley, Daddy and I were walking to the corrals on his farm to feed the cows. Daddy slipped on his worn-out leather gloves and looked at me. "I've noticed that you and Mark never do things together."

So it was that obvious. I stared straight ahead. "Yip, you're right Daddy." Just by Daddy's observations, he helped me to recognize an aspect of my marriage that I had simply accepted as the norm.

Now, my bull—a symbol of regenerative energy—refused to enter the house. Once I became aware of this dynamic, I was able to move in.

One day, Daddy helped me move the trash barrels farther away from the house. I was afraid that the wind might catch a flame and cause a fire. After Daddy left, I was resting in the bedroom when Mark walked in. He pushed the door open and yelled, "Why did you move those barrels without talking to me first? And why did you have your father help you?"

"Because I was afraid the flames might jump the lane and start the house on fire. It's not a big deal." How could he harass me about those barrels? Maybe I should have asked him first, but the thought did not enter my mind. I was reaching my limit with his irrational behavior.

It seemed the more stress there was, the more difficult Mark became. For the last two years, change had dominated our lives with my encounter with the Black Madonna and all that entailed, our selling the computer graphics company, and our moving to Colorado. Here, we were left without our professions that gave us security, and our foundation was crumbling. For years, we were caught in a whirlwind of careers, and suddenly we landed in Colorado without the tools to build a new future together. It appeared that this house renovation failed to include an insulation of trust and openness to bring forth new possibilities.

Our patience with each other steadily diminished. To take a break, I left with Marissa and Andrea for the Oregon coast to spend a month in our beach house. There I walked the speckled sand for miles searching for a bottle washed onto the beach that had a message for our troubled marriage. But no matter how much I searched, nothing appeared on the sand. If I thought my life had fallen apart when we left Seattle, any remaining fragments were now fine dust.

When I returned from Cannon Beach, I had convinced

myself that somehow, someway I would remain in the marriage with conditions. At night, I slept on a couch upstairs instead of sleeping with Mark. One time during the night Mark walked upstairs. He sat at the end of the couch. "Come downstairs and sleep with me."

"No, I want to sleep here." I felt I had to remain strong and determined, or I would get drawn into our old routine. Mark appeared bewildered but yielded to my need.

One night I had the following dream:

October 2, 1988

It is early morning light and I'm (sleeping) on the couch upstairs. I hear (Mark) typing on the keyboard.

Sleeping – unaware of something

Then I hear him walking upstairs. He approaches me and puts his hands around my neck, and he tries to strangle me.

Who is Mark in my own psyche that is strangling me?

I jump up and start running downstairs. He grabs a (kitty) bowl and throws it at me. As I am running out of the house, he catches me.

Kitty – symbol for the Feminine

Just as I turn the doorknob, he grabs my neck and begins to strangle me.

I wake up trying to scream, but I don't have a (voice).

As much as I want to talk about problems, I am fearful to express my feelings.

When awakened, I was lying on the couch. I was confused whether I was awake or whether was I still sleeping. Then I heard Mark downstairs tapping on the computer keyboard.

I was still in the experience of the dream where I was unable to talk. My words and sounds were being held prisoners in my throat. Terrified, I quietly walked down the staircase until I passed Mark's office. I opened the front door and ran into the night to the guesthouse where my sister Ann and her husband lived. I knocked on the door. They opened it.

"I need to sleep on your couch."

They glanced at each other but simply said, "Sure."

Trembling, I snuggled into the soft blanket on the couch and eventually fell asleep. The dream triggered fear that challenged me to reevaluate my decision to stay in the marriage. Later, I worked on the symbols of the dream:

Early morning light — an awakening, consciousness

Sleeping — unconscious about something

Hands around my neck and tries to strangle me — my inability (symbolized by Mark) to have a voice (like the incident with V&V and the stick of wood barring any expression of my emotions)

Kitty bowl — the young Feminine; bowl, container of the Feminine; kitty, often associated with independence, mystery, and unpredictability

Voice — expression, communication

When I reflected on the dream, I had many realizations. For decades, I had imprisoned my voice, because it was easier to be the observer whose thoughts and perceptions were protected. I valued being the obedient daughter, as well as the obedient wife.

Daddy was a strong Masculine force that continually gave me love and support. I found myself agreeing with his ideas and the opinions of other strong men, because I wanted to receive their acceptance and love. This pattern continued with Mark. I knew our problems were as much about my issues as they were about him.

It was easy to yield to Mark's intelligence, but he had emotional scars from his mother's death and his father's absence while he served in the military. He rarely dealt with these issues of loss.

I should have said to Mark, "You need to deal with your

anger, especially with women. I don't deserve your fury. You've got to figure out where your moodiness comes from."

The night of the dream was the last night I spent in our house. I told Mark, "We need to separate to figure things out."

He was not surprised. "That sounds okay."

I knew we needed to tell Marissa and Andrea. We sat at the kitchen table. "Girls, your father and I are going to live separately. We've agreed that you'll stay with me during the week, and on the weekends you'll be with your father."

They stayed quiet.

I moved into my parents' house until I was able to rent a cottage-like house that the girls and I liked.

The separation almost killed me, because it went against everything I believed in. When I was twenty-two years old, I had vowed to stay married for a lifetime. Seven of my aunts were Catholic nuns who had committed collectively over 350 years to God. In our family, other people got divorces, not us. I never wanted to be a divorcee, and I never wanted my children to be the victims of a broken marriage. I thought, *If God was so powerful, why was he incapable of fixing our marriage?* Daily, I prayed and meditated as if the rosary beads were a lifeline pulling me out of drowning waters. Words of Thomas Merton sustained me while I endured this violent storm.

My Lord God, I have no idea where I am going.

. . .Therefore I will trust you always though I may seem to be lost and in the shadow of death. I will not fear, for you are ever with me, and you will never leave me to face my perils alone.

When the mountains of grief came tumbling down, I was left with the stark reality that we had failed to nourish the love that had brought us together. I had ignored the needs of my heart for closeness and happiness. I treated love as if it were an object that could be stored away in a drawer. But I realized that our love was the rose in the yard that needed water, rich soil, and sunlight in order to blossom.

After six months of looking at some options like marriage counseling, I realized I lacked the motivation and determination to work on our relationship. After years of neglect, my feelings had withered and died. I finally saw the brutal truth of my situation. I filed for a divorce.

Months later, after the divorce hearing, Mark and I met outside in the middle of the courtyard where we hugged and cried. I would always love Mark. But I knew that if we lacked the courage to overcome our parting, our relationship would remain sterile and bitter. Now, the unlived parts of our personalities were free to grow.

Chapter Eleven

THE HEALING GIFT OF LISTENING WITH THE HEART

Listening was the basis of my relationship with the Black Madonna. Our relationship was initiated when I asked her, "What do you want me to hear?" But sometimes, I became too introverted and comfortable in the peacefulness that I found in prayer and in meditation to be attentive to others. I forgot to make listening a priority in my relationships with my family, friends, and neighbors. It was important to be attentive to my dreams, my feelings, and my intuition, but equally as important was listening to people and their longing to be heard.

I was reminded of this necessity when I attended a lecture given by Dr. Ursula Wirtz, a Jungian analyst, who lectured on "Listening to the Wounded Soul." In English with a German accent, Dr. Wirtz stood at the lectern and faced a room filled with participants. She began: "A missionary arrives in a desert with a Bedouin. Suddenly, the Bedouin gets off his camel and puts his ear to the sand and listens.

'What are you doing?' asks the missionary.

And the Bedouin says 'I am listening. I hear the desert weeping. It wants to become a garden.'"

Dr. Wirtz had just returned from Bosnia where she had supervised psychologists who worked with traumatized children and women who had been mass raped in the refugee camps.

"How can the victims be healed? How can we help them return from the realm of the dead to the land of the living?" she asked the audience.

She suggested that healing could be done through a particular type of listening. It is listening with the heart to what wants to be born.

She said, "Regular meditation and symbols can help us become good midwives. They link us to our inner strength and provide safety and a sense of boundaries. And with this strength we can listen to the questions of suffering and give it meaning."

Dr. Wirtz inspired me to be a good midwife who would help create a world of healing. In order to accomplish this, I needed to renew my abilities as an astute listener who offered a receptive ear with a gesture of compassion.

For years, the discipline of meditation and working with dreams had improved my ability to be present to my inner voice. The subtle sounds of Nature, like sandhill cranes flying through the sky, the breeze swirling dried leaves, or the soft landing of a snowflake also helped me to refine my listening skills.

During my marital separation, Marissa, Andrea, and I were living in a small cottage on a farm about ten miles from Capulin when I had the following dream:

October 5, 1988

I'm in a delicatessen in (Capulin). I'm (serving) fish and meat from behind a glass display counter.	Capulin: a Hispanic community three miles west of my home serving food

When I associated to the symbols, "serving" had the biggest charge. I continued to dig deeper in my beloved dictionary, which revealed that the story for the word "delicatessen" came from Latin *delicates*, delicate. The definition for "delicate" was "regardful of the feelings of others." I realized that I needed to be sensitive to others and to my newfound Hispanic community, Capulin, which involved some type of service. Capulin in Spanish means "chokecherry," a small maroon berry grown in tall willow-like bushes that are native to this area. Mom used their tart juices to make scrumptious jam and syrup while others used them to make wine. I wondered what other delicacies were in store for this community.

Although, I still saw myself as an outsider who had moved from the big city of Seattle, in spite of having been raised so near here. I had been gone for close to twenty years. I remembered many people, some who were distant relatives, who attended church. I had kept a polite distance. I might say, "How are you doing?" or "Nice day, huh?" or "Heard about your loss, so sorry."

In my formative years, I never felt I belonged to any town. I was sheltered, living on the family farm that met most of my personal nutritional needs; eating our home-grown steaks, eggs gathered from the chicken coop, and vegetables grown in Mom's garden; socializing with cousins; and babysitting for relatives to earn spending money to buy mascara. Of course, there was some connection to the outside world through attending public school, worshipping at Saint Joseph Catholic Church, and doing some shopping in the nearby towns of Alamosa and La Jara.

I knew that building relationships within a community took time. Many of these skills I had used in my psychotherapeutic practice, but now with a warm heart I was taking them into my everyday relationships. I wanted to make each person feel they were the most important person in my life, like what Daddy was able to do. This built trust. While talking to people, I turned off my cell phone, because the calls were too much of a distraction. I strove for transparency. In conversations, I owned up to my confusion and asked for clarity. Pretending that I was listening was unacceptable.

A few months later, after the divorce, the girls and I moved a couple of miles east of Capulin. I bought a small adobe house that my great-uncle, *Tio* Polito, with Dad's help, had built around 1930. The ten acres of land that surrounded our house gave Marissa and Andrea plenty of space to play. In early spring I loved falling asleep with the window open with a cool breeze blanketing me, and listening to rippling sounds from the *acequia* (dirt ditch) that circled our house.

When I drove into Capulin, it was hard to ignore the cemetery, spread over four acres of land, that was a few feet from the main road. The graveyard was enclosed by a white picket fence. One day, I decided to stop. I parked my car and walked through the gate. At the center of the cemetery was a twenty-foot-high wooden cross with a statue of a crucified Christ. The cross was made of white sand, which was brought from New Mexico in the 1940s. Kneeling below Jesus were the figures of Mary Magdalene, Jesus's mother Mary, and his mother's sister Mary.

When I saw the cross, I instantly became melancholic. Only months ago, I had encountered my cross which had transformed my life into serving the spiritual realm. It was a painful process, but a necessary one in which my ego had surrendered to the Divine.

I never enjoyed visiting cemeteries and talking about death and its sadness. I was certainly Grandpa Juanito's granddaughter. Grandpa was able to dodge death for over 100 years.

In Seattle, raising two busy toddlers, dealing with the chaos of the new company, and working with clients helped me avoid the topic of death. I was too much in the throes of living and too naive to think about it outside the counseling room. Since I had moved back to the Valley, I had attended two to three funerals a month, much more than the total of four funerals I had attended in the Pacific Northwest. Weeks ago, when Andrea and I drove past this cemetery, she looked out the car window. "Mommy, we need to plant flowers and trees in our cemetery plot, so that it'll be ready for us."

Andrea had an innovative idea: actually plan for death. During meditation, I found time to listen to Death. I heard: "I claim everyone. Age is irrelevant. I am the portal everyone must pass through."

There were no guarantees about what would happen after I died, but I believed that the intuitive world of the Feminine would guide me. In the vision of Christ standing on the clouds and bowing down and kissing my hand, a synergy of tenderness and strength radiated through me. At that sacred moment, polarities ceased to exist, creating a new reality. When Christ pointed to his Sacred Heart, I was reminded that I had to embody love and compassion in every step I took. And I was convinced those steps would be the pathway to the everlasting.

I continued walking through the cemetery. The granite headstones reminded me of book covers waiting to be flipped open to the lives of these women and men. I stood in front of two stone pillars, etched with crosses and flowers, that read:

Ramonsita G   Encarnacion
Romero   Romero

1877-1952   1860-1945

Great-grandma Ramoncita's name had been misspelled on her headstone. The *c* had been spelled with a *s* as it had sounded. Ramoncita and Encarnacion were my paternal great-grandparents. I was in Mom's womb when great-grandma Ramoncita died. Our paths almost crossed.

As a young boy, Daddy said he often spent the night with Papa Mero (Grandpa Encarnacion), a sheepherder, whose eyes were grayish-blue and hair, curly black, and who often said with a sigh, "*Bendito sea Dios* (blessed be God)." Mama Tita (Grandma Ramoncita) often dressed with a feathered hat, earrings, and a necklace when she left after supper to pray the rosary for relatives. In addition, she often had to walk over ten miles to reach their homes. Before she left, she baked Daddy's favorite white cake with thick jelly between the layers.

Daddy said that while Mama Tita was away, Papa Mero started story time by whispering about nights with only the stars twinkling and the campfire crackling. Daddy was swallowed up by the eerie landscape of ghosts and superstition.

Grandpa Mero began, "One night while the crescent moon was above my sheepherder's camp, I heard the dogs barking. I jumped on the horse to check the sheep while *hermano* (brother) Guillermo stayed asleep in the tent. When I returned a half hour later, *hermano* was gone. I looked for him around the campfire, behind the aspen trees, but he wasn't anywhere. Was it the Utes who had stolen him, or was it a mountain lion that dragged him away?" In fact, h*ermano* Guillermo was never seen again.

After a fitful night, the next morning Daddy was awakened by the soft morning light as it filtered through the curtains. He heard his grandparents honor the new day with their angelic voices:

O Maria, Madre mia, o Consuelo del mortal

Amparadme y guiadme a la patria celestial

(O Mary, my mother, our mortal consolation

Protect me and guide me to the celestial homeland)

I was grateful that Daddy shared these memories of his grandparents with me. In a sense, I felt I had met them.

In the cemetery, attached to many of the headstones were small American flags waving in the breeze that tagged men and women who fought as warriors. Daddy, who was a proud Marine, epitomized a unique breed of men whose wounds left blood on foreign soil while fighting during World War II (WWII), part of a league of men and women who journalist and author Tom Brokaw referred to as the "greatest generation." These soldiers returned home from exotic countries with wounds sutured with threads of trauma, wisdom, and indomitable strength.

I remembered visiting Uncle Adelmo, a WWII veteran. He had attended national conferences for WWII veterans. He always talked about the war and how one day he woke up in a hospital bed in France. "When I came back from the war I wasn't right. When I returned home, I herded my sheep up to the mountains. I wasn't sure I'd be coming back." His eyes filled with tears.

I pushed my chair closer to him, "Oh, Uncle." I could not imagine the physical and psychological trauma he carried.

With a smirk he said, "I spent the entire summer with the sheep in those mountains. Being alone up there helped me to heal."

I was not surprised that those snowcapped mountains —with their lush valleys and herds of elk and sprinkled with purple and yellow columbine flowers—were able to heal a wounded soul.

I looked around in the cemetery at the headstones of the great men and women who had made unbelievable sacrifices when they rode their horses into this New Frontier from northern Mexico. They had no idea of the poverty and hard work they would have to confront. The unknowns did not stop them. They had cleared hundreds of cottonwood trees so they could build their homes. Then they made the ultimate sacrifice of fighting in wars for the people they loved. It was time for me to embrace the rich Hispanic culture that had birthed me. I realized that richness came in different forms and that one of my greatest treasures was connecting to my cultural legacy which, in turn, would reconnect me to the people in Capulin.

With a deep breath of inspiration, I left the cemetery and walked to the car. I drove toward Capulin. On the horizon were the San Juan Mountains, rising to 13,000 feet, capped with over 200 inches of snow during a normal winter season. The mountains were a haven for hunters, fishermen, and gatherers of wood and berries, like the Utes who called it home.

Lining the highway were adobe houses and mobile homes, adorned with stacks of wood. Eddie's Bar, Bernie's Shearing Shack, Malouff's Grocery Store, Junior's Repair Shop, the post office that was uniquely painted a green sherbet color, and many vacant businesses filled this landscape. In this isolated area, vestiges of seventeenth century Spanish, such as *provisiones* and *roñoso,* were still spoken.

One block from the main road I saw a cross on top of the church that identified Saint Joseph Church. The 1912 sandstone edifice was built by hard-working people like my grandfathers, Juanito and Felipe, who used horse-drawn wagons to haul rock from a nearby quarry. Across the street was a two-story red brick school that many people built, brick by brick, through the Work Projects Administration (WPA) created by President Franklin D. Roosevelt. Threaded through the outskirts of town was the Alamosa River, a seasonal river that irrigated thousands of acres of land. Over several months, in conversations with people around town, I heard:

"We need a place for recreation."

"A youth center for social events is needed."

"A community center would be great."

During my training in Process-oriented Psychology in Switzerland, I was taught how to trust the clients' innate wisdom and how to follow their process. I now transferred this knowledge to the residents of Capulin, who knew better than anyone else what their town needed and what direction should be taken. These men and women had little need for power and were able to look beyond their own egos. I invited four men and four women who were responsible, caring, and loving people to be cofounders of a community center; they became its first board of directors.

Forming a nonprofit community center emerged from several meetings. In the United States, the federal Internal Revenue Service provides a mechanism to form grassroots organizations with a mission to help alleviate the burden of government, and, in doing so, provides an infrastructure for creative projects. The infrastructure was important: mission statement, by-laws, budget, and adherence to the legality of our nonprofit classification. Our mission statement read that the center "promotes the dignity and value of life through programs which assist each person to develop their inner assets, thus becoming a creative and valuable contributor to the community and to society." A CPA offered his pro bono services to write and submit our application for our federal 501(c)(3) designation. Our application was approved, and we received a not-for-profit status.

At first, there was lots of excitement and hopefulness about this new venture. In retrospect, the board should have spent more time critiquing the by-laws of the organization. Several attorneys should have reviewed these governing rules in order to make them as strong as possible. In our brevity, the by-laws were weak. Our laxity would haunt us years later when future board members allowed their desire for power to override the by-laws. Instead of saying "*our* community center," power driven individuals said, "*my* community center." Unfortunately, legal action was required to resolve these ownership problems.

In the beginning, however, all nine of the board of directors met in a little cafeteria that was part of the community center. We sat around an old wooden table. The budget was discussed, and Barbara, our treasurer, looked hopeless.

"Just for operating expenses we need at least $5,000 a year. Where are we going to find this money?"

"Maybe fundraisers," Lela suggested.

"How about submitting an application to a foundation?" someone else said.

Father Rudy said, "Our order can loan you $5,000 until you can find the money."

A motion was made to accept this loan and to repay it as soon as possible. The motion unanimously passed.

After the meeting, I took my concerns, self-doubts, and questions about finding funds into my meditative practice. In the silent darkness, I was forced to think differently. I surrendered to the idea that I was not in control, a challenge I continuously worked on. Before long, in that darkness, I began to think about learning how to write grants. Surely, if I had written a thesis in graduate school, I could learn how to write a grant application. In the following weeks, I read all I could about funders, then talked to other grant writers. Before I knew it, our applications were accepted, and we hosted fundraisers to pay back Father Rudy's loan.

Author Andrew Harvey coined the term "mystical activism." According to the Andrew Harvey Institute for Sacred Activism™, "Sacred Activism is a transforming force of compassion-in-action that is born of a fusion of deep spiritual knowledge, courage, love and passion, with wise radical action in the world." This concept fused mysticism and activism, which to me seemed mutually exclusive. Yet, many of my aunts were Catholic nuns and served in Peru, Columbia, the Fiji Islands, and in various parts of the United States. They lived in a religious order and then were activists in the world. Prayer was an integral part of their lives. One summer, Sister Rebecca came home for respite and told us, "Columbia is a violent country. I hear gunshots throughout the night. I know I'm going to be killed there. Some nights I have so many nightmares, I can't sleep. Finally, I realized that if I die there, it was my destiny."

I refrained from asking Sister Rebecca how many prayers that realization had required, but I bet it was a lot. Surrendering to the Divine's direction was a continuous process.

I preferred to think of Sacred Activism as mystical activism. This concept offered a paradigm to help bring understanding into my lifestyle and work. My meditation and activism depended on each other, and they infused passion and energy into my work, especially during challenging times.

Initially, some people to whom I talked about the community center said, "Why work with this place that has so many drug and alcohol problems?"

Other naysayers added:

"The community center will never work."

"No one will help you."

"You'll never be able to find the money."

People's negativity drained my energy and dropped a heavy black curtain over our vision. Their negativity constellated my own self-doubts. *What am I doing? Where in my background was there any nonprofit experience? My education was in psychology, not community development.*

And the Oregon beach was still calling me. I longed for the tranquility of walking on the beach at sunset and watching the pink and maroon colors across the horizon reflect on the beach. I yearned to read my books as I relaxed inside the beach house, looking out the picture window at the crashing waves. In meditation, I bartered with the Black Madonna:

I could find community work on the Oregon coast. Surely, a community center was needed there.

Silence. There was not an experience, a feeling, or an intuitive impulse to confirm my request. No, my destiny remained in the Valley where I would learn how to embody this mystical activism.

Capulin had little economic or political clout. Demographics categorized Capulin as being located in one of the poorest counties in the nation. Although the people who lived here were our most valuable assets. Their human qualities of compassion, commitment, and sharing of time and gifts were as important as money or any impressive educational degrees. Carpenters, cooks, electricians, and plumbers volunteered their expertise and time to support the community center. We were all cofounders of the center.

The community center also served as a think tank for creative ideas and for sharing talents. One day Marlene approached me with the idea of starting a folklorico dance troupe that used traditional Mexican music. She was a former folklorico dancer and would be the perfect teacher and mentor. I thought this program would be easy to implement, and it would give Marissa, Andrea, and me an opportunity to share a fun activity. I could help with the public relations, and Marlene could teach the class. Marissa and Andrea, as well as many other girls who ranged in ages from seven to thirteen years old, joined the dance troupe. Their mothers sewed their skirts that each required ten yards of material. The young dancers looked dramatic with their dark hair tied in buns as they swirled their bright red floral skirts. Practices were longer and more demanding as *Cinco de Mayo* festivities were quickly approaching. Eventually, the dancers performed in eight different schools over two days.

"They look just like butterflies," said an admiring fan.

Ideas continued to spark. Debbie, a mother in the community, said, "We need to help our kids with their education." This geographical area had one of the highest dropout rates in the school district. I was uncertain where to find financial help to start this tutoring program. I soon learned that building relationships outside the community was as important as connections within the community. A friend suggested that the presidents' offices at the University of Colorado and Colorado State University might fund this project. I contacted them, and they funded our tutoring program and gave us technical support in implementing the program. Then parents and teenagers were recruited to listen to the children read. Volunteers and parents made sure the children's homework was completed and assured them that, even though an education was not easy to attain, it was necessary. As we became more successful, our financial resources increased to include a $365,000 domestic violence initiative.

My ancestors continuously served as inspiration. If they could build a church using horse-drawn wagons, certainly I could be creative enough to think of ways to raise money. They were people of faith, which motivated them to work together for the betterment of their community. And so was I.

Chapter Twelve

Environmental Stewardship

I was flying high knowing that thirty-five kids, including Marissa and Andrea, were participating in the community center's summer day camp, and group and individual guitar lessons were being scheduled. I had no inkling that a heinous act was taking place at 12,000 feet elevation in the San Juan Mountains.

Unexpectedly, a metal sign was posted at the Alamosa Campground, just west of Capulin:

RIVER WATER CONTAMINATED

BY HEAVY METALS

DO NOT DRINK

This was meant to warn residents and tourists of the environmental devastation in the Alamosa River watershed. A telephone call helped me to recognize what had happened to the river. "Cindy, can you participate in the Technical Assistance

Grant? We need people to serve on this committee. Summitville was designated a Superfund site," said my neighbor Alice.

"What are you talking about?" Summitville, I knew, was a gold mine high in the San Juan Mountains that was now abandoned. Or so I thought.

"Haven't you seen the fish floating in the river? The farmers have dead fish in their ponds, too. At the Summitville mine site there was a cyanide spill, and, with the combination of heavy metals, the Alamosa River was contaminated."

My mind was incapable of absorbing these horrendous details; so to slow the pace, I responded, "Let me think about it. I'll call you back." My feelings were similar to those when I was in Switzerland and first heard about the Chernobyl catastrophe. These bitter words were hard to swallow.

The Alamosa River was used for irrigation and was essential to the lives of ranchers and farmers who lived in the Valley. The river water was never pure, but somehow fish were able to tolerate the heavy metals seeping from old mine sites and metal-laden mountains. Stunner Camp, a recreational area, showcased mountains glistening in gold and silvery pink. It was the norm for the water to shimmer with a tinge of brownish-orange, especially during spring runoff. But the discoloration never stopped Mom from catching fish there.

In 1988, five years ago when I had returned to the Valley from Seattle, the Alamosa River was where I had meditated for hours while sitting on a blanket of grass under the filigree canopy of cottonwood branches, surrounded by wild lavender irises. I was entertained by fish chasing each other around the bare tree roots that were submerged in the water. The currents cascading over rocks and drumming the embankment was my private symphony. Nature had brought tranquility into my chaotic life while I was integrating my spiritual experiences and embodying this new Feminine perspective into my life.

My memories took me further back to when I was a kid who hid in the tall alfalfa fields, a natural fortress that protected me from all the evils of the world, who at the time were my bossy older sisters, Vivien and Veronica. Nature was my magical kingdom where I instantly felt secure and entertained.

And now the unbelievable had happened. The river water was toxic for humans, fish, and vegetation. In essence, we had a dead river. How could this have happened? Who could have been so irresponsible to cause such a disaster? I could not fit all the pieces together. And then I, who had nothing to do with this catastrophe, was supposed to help in the reclamation efforts.

I had some considerations to think about. Where was I going to find time to attend more meetings? My two active pre-adolescents with their homework, sports events, and dance—as well as my involvement with the community center—left little time for anything else. I was resentful about this predicament where I had to choose between spending time with my family or working on this fiasco. To bolster my position, I convinced myself that I lacked the appropriate credentials to be on this committee, because my field of study was psychology, not geology or biology. It was one thing to learn about community development, but it was another thing to get involved with complex environmental issues that I knew nothing about. My answer was going to be, "I don't have time to participate. I wish you the best of luck."

Before I telephoned my neighbor, I retreated into my inner refuge where I reflected and prayed to either receive confirmation on my decision or to be open to a new direction. After meditating, I opened my eyes, and in front of me was the icon of the Black Madonna hanging on the wall. The Madonna's dark face became the dark soil where I saw a farmer plowing and preparing his rich land for planting. It was as if the Madonna had become the earth. I could not separate her from the land and its people. Everyone was dependent on the river.

My insights continued. Nature had greatly influenced my formative years. I grew up on a farm where my parents instilled a work ethic in me. And I felt the earth's support when I was going through my divorce. A few days before our court hearing, I sat on a log next to the river, where I was reminded that the God of Snow and Rain, who gave blessings to this river, would also provide for me. Now, Nature desperately needed my voice to bring healing to this irreplaceable natural system.

I protested, "Noooooooooo!" As if I could say "no" to the Black Madonna. Even though I was moving forward, I was aware of my resistance and resentfulness.

I stood up from my meditation and walked to the phone. "Hi, Alice. I've decided to be a member of the committee. Let me know about the next meeting."

"Actually, Governor Romer is visiting Capulin next week to talk about what happened at Summitville. If you have time, you might attend."

"Okay, let me see if the girls can stay with Mom and Dad."

My children, as well as many others, would sacrifice family time for this clean up. As a single mother, I was depending on my parents and my sisters to help me with Marissa and Andrea, so I could be available for the meetings.

On Monday, May 10, 1993, Colorado's Governor Romer met with about 200 people at the gym at the community center. I sat in the bleachers waiting for the meeting to start. As the locals were finding a place to sit, I overheard conversations:

"How bad do you think the river is? Should I be worried about my alfalfa?"

"Who knows? Let's see if these politicians know anything."

"Have you seen the river? I wouldn't put my toe in it. It's as thick as orange mud."

"What the hell was the government thinking? What a bunch of asses! Why weren't they monitoring the site like they were supposed to?"

Governor Romer walked to the microphone in front of the agitated crowd. He explained in a reassuring way that on December 16, 1992, Summitville Consolidated Mining Company, Inc., a subsidiary of Galactic Resources Ltd. of British Columbia, Canada, had declared bankruptcy. When the Environmental Protection Agency (EPA) intervened, they found an "appalling situation." The construction of the heap leach pad had been completed irresponsibly. Financial resources were needed to clean up the mess. The governor said that $15 million of Superfund monies had been made available.

Then, the governor introduced blue-suited representatives from the Colorado Department of Public Health and Environment, Colorado Department of Natural Resources, and the EPA. Tim, the EPA liaison, said that the project was listed on the Superfund national priority list. The governor announced that a geologist, Dr. Harold, would be in the Valley as a liaison to his office. Romer reassured us that a major cleanup of the site would be completed, and, most importantly, another disaster would never happen again.

In my naiveté, I thought Governor Romer was nice to fly to the Valley to assure us of state and federal assistance.

When I picked up Marissa and Andrea, I said, "I need to take a ride to the mountains. Do you want to go?"

"Sure, Mom. Do you think we can go fishing?"

"No, Andrea, I'm sorry that we can't go fishing there anymore. Some company from Canada released cyanide with the combination of heavy metals into the river and killed all the fish."

"But I have a new fishing pole that Daddy bought me."

"I know. Maybe sometime we can go fishing above Summitville or in Creede."

Then Marissa piped up. "Mom, this is sad. Why would someone want to kill the fish?"

"This Canadian company was mining for gold, and they supposedly used a state-of-the-art process that totally failed. I think we should take a ride to Summitville to see for ourselves." They agreed.

One Sunday after Mass, I gathered a bag of barbecue chips, packed leftover baked chicken and chocolate chip cookies, poured ice tea in a thermos, and loaded everything in the car. With Marissa and Andrea, I drove up above Stunner Camp to Summitville. Snowbanks were melting, and mud was everywhere.

"Oh, Mom, this road is terrible. It's so muddy and so

bumpy. Do you think we're going to make it?" Marissa said holding onto her seat belt.

"I should have borrowed Daddy's truck. Just hold on. We have maybe another hour. I didn't realize the road had so many potholes. I hope I don't bust a tire."

Finally, I saw Summitville and parked the car. The site was surrounded by a high metal fence with a locked gate. But the environmental disaster could be seen from anywhere. Trailers and long pipes that looked like snakes covered the ground. Once a cornucopia of wildlife roamed these green velvet-covered mountains; now the ailing landscape of barren rock looked like a decimated corpse. Half of South Mountain was gone. Later, I learned that this mountain had been crushed into ore, leaving an exposed mountain bleeding with iron, zinc, aluminum, and copper. The unprotected rock, when exposed to oxygen and precipitation, created acid mining drainage that destroyed everything in its path, which included aquatic life and vegetation. It was as if tons of battery acid had spilled from the mountain into the Alamosa River.

Andrea asked, "Mom, what happened to the mountain? It looks like they had a big knife and cut half the mountain off. It's so ugly here, and it's so cold. Let's go home." She turned and walked back to the car.

It was unfathomable to me that any mining company would start construction at 12,000 feet elevation during a winter that received over 400 inches of snow. Any type of material would freeze. And that is exactly what happened when they tried to construct a large scale, open pit, cyanide heap leach pad. They excavated the land for a pond-like pit that required an impermeable liner. Crushed low grade ore was poured into this pond, then the ore was peppered with cyanide to extract the gold. The *impermeable* liner tore, leaking cyanide and heavy metals. The mining company had too much untreated water; so, without a permit, they sprayed the untreated water that contained cyanide and metals on the surrounding land. The deadly mixture eventually reached Wightman Fork, a tributary to the Alamosa River. The cyanide dissipated within the first few miles, but the heavy metals of copper and iron reached the Alamosa River.

This deplorable destructiveness and dishonor to the earth was in complete contrast to the history of the area. The Ute Indians had inhabited millions of acres in the San Juan Mountains. To traditional people of this land that I, too, loved, the earth was a living entity, and its heartbeat pulsed in special rocks on sacred peaks. Unfortunately, the defacement of South Mountain silenced its vibration.

Chief Ouray and his fellow Utes depended on the San Juans—especially in the summer and early fall—for hunting elk, deer, and rabbit; for gathering roots, nuts, and berries; and for fishing. I could identify with the Utes. Grandma Rosana had gathered herbs for healing in these mountains. These trees had provided wood in the form of dead branches that were gathered and used as our only source of heat during the frigid winter months. The fish, elk, and deer had fed our family, too. Grandma stored *carne seca* (dried deer meat), as well as *piñon* (pine) nuts, in empty white flour sacks.

Now Marissa agreed with her sister. "Mom, let's go. It's cold and too ugly here."

I started the ignition, and we drove away from this environmental tragedy.

In the following weeks, an onslaught of meetings with the state and the EPA began. The meetings were mostly held at the kitchen of the community center. We gathered around a well-worn table as if for decades we had been one big happy family eating enchiladas. The state project manager was Amanda, who was as thin as a pencil. The EPA project manager, Tim, was laid back and approachable. Unfortunately, Dr. Harold, the liaison for Governor Romer's office, attended sporadically. Alice was our local project administrator. Consultants and committee members sat around the rectangular table.

The goal of the grant was to disseminate information about the Superfund process to the local residents. The goal was simple enough, but the data's technical language, abbreviations, and acronyms left me two steps behind in every discussion. Technical language like "metal loadings," "altered mineralized areas," UAA, IROS, and IR/FS created a communication schism in spite of the technical consultant the EPA had provided. Then we had to review different remediations for the site, as well as issues concerning the high acidic discharges from the Reynolds Tunnel. There was not enough space in my home office for all the technical documents and paperwork.

After one meeting, Alice and I walked together to our cars. I lowered my voice. "Can you believe how arrogant Dr. Harold is? It's hard to ask questions when he's so condescending and sarcastic. I tend to back down."

Alice stopped and moved closer. "Well, the state doesn't have any reason to be arrogant. Did you hear that they were supposed to be monitoring the heap leach pad; but, because the state's budget was cut, they eliminated the additional inspectors that were desperately needed?"

I looked at the Catholic Church across the street and remembered all the men and women who built that church almost 100 years ago. I could only admire the focus and precision needed to cut the quarry rock for the walls. Too bad Galactic lacked their superb work ethic.

Alice kept talking. The Colorado Mined Land Reclamation Board initially rejected Galactic's mining permit only to be overridden by the Colorado State Legislature. Then the legislature decided that all permits must be evaluated within six months or they're automatically approved. Can you believe that crap?"

"No!"

"Yes! If Colorado wasn't so friendly with the mining industry, they would've been more thorough with the permitting process and demanded a bigger bond."

"You mean to tell me that the state could've avoided this disaster?"

"You got it, girl."

I shook my head in disbelief. "I need to go. I'll talk to you later."

As I was driving home I thought about how gullible I had been. I had totally trusted the government to always protect me and other citizens, no matter what the situation was. I felt betrayed, and everyone knows that there are very few things worse than betrayal. My misplaced trust had turned into anger and resentment.

That night as I was getting into bed, I picked up a book on Chief Ouray. For years, Chief Ouray fought for the Treaty of 1868 that was supposed to prevent any white man from walking on their land. A tug-of-war ensued for several years. The Utes demanded that the federal government remove the trespassers who were panning for gold and silver. For Chief Ouray, a man had only his word. But as gold and silver strikes erupted throughout the Territory of Colorado, the gold and silver fever ran too hot and eventually burned any source of commitment to the Utes.

Perhaps Chief Ouray saw the inevitability of the situation, which prompted him to sign the Brunot Treaty on September 13, 1873, that pushed the Utes farther west and onto a smaller piece of land for their hunting and fishing.

This treaty opened the doors for the Summitville Mining District. Prospectors from around the world invaded the mountains. Chief Ouray, known for his peaceful ways, could not have imagined that over 100 years later, the San Juan Mountains that once fed his people would be decimated by a negligent Canadian-owned mining company and a government that continued to renege on its promises to its people. On that low note, I turned off the night-light.

At the next meeting, Isidro, another community member, was on the war path about the United State General Mining Law of 1872. This law had conveniently passed one year before the Utes were driven out of their land. Isidro placed his cowboy hat on his knee. Then, he pounded his fist on the table. "We need to get rid of this antiquated General Mining Law of 1872 that allows anyone to buy public land for five dollars an acre for its minerals, like gold. I'm tired of these mining companies not paying any royalties or fees for these minerals. The taxpayer is getting screwed while the mining companies are getting fatter. I'm fed up with this injustice. When are the taxpayers going to say 'the buck stops here?'"

Amanda, the state project manager, interrupted, "We're

not here to talk about this law. You'll have to take it up with your congressman. There's some water quality data that we have to review."

"You should care about this. It's condoning miners who are using public land for mining projects that are destroying our natural resources."

Amanda sighed and persisted. "We've got a lot of data to cover."

Eventually, Isidro and other people in Colorado took on the challenge of changing this out-of-date legislation. Of course, opposition from mining companies made it difficult to amend the law.

Gil piped up, "You keep saying there weren't any fish in the river, but we have anecdotal data that many people in this town caught fish in the river prior to this accident."

"Well, no one sufficiently documented any fish data." Amanda responded as she paced back and forth.

I was thinking, *Ask my Mom, and she'd say, "Wrong! I've eaten more fish from the river than you could count."*

Gil, who was sitting next to me, mumbled while his long mustache almost scratched my cheek. "Other people living in watershed areas have to learn from this catastrophe. Citizens must gather baseline data about their river and watersheds, so that if a disaster happens—God forbid—they'll have data to use for liability issues."

"Kinda like taking an inventory of your house: in case there's a fire or a theft, you'll know what needs to be replaced."

"Exactly!"

After we left the meeting that lasted four hours, Alice gathered us outside in the parking lot. "I've had film crews from the BBC, CBS, and CNN, as well as from New Zealand and Norway, contact me. Will some of you meet with them to talk about Summitville?"

"I guess I can talk to one or two people," I offered.

"Good, I'll be calling you when they get into town. And I'll be calling the rest of you to see if you're available or not. Thanks."

Within a few weeks, I met a reporter from New Zealand at the river. Earlier I had realized that I had to step up and be more vocal about this environmental travesty. My Pollyanna attitude was a way of colluding with the mining company. I would hate to see another community go through the stress and despair at losing their viable natural resources like we had.

The reporter asked, "What about this Robert Friedland, who was CEO of the company?"

"I consider Robert Friedland an environmental rapist. He could have cared less about the fish or the land. All he cared about was making money to pay back his loans. He crushed the mountain into oblivion, destroying everything in his path. If he did it here, he's capable of repeating it in New Zealand and everywhere else in the world. You have to protect your rivers and bays from this unconscionable man."

Sadly, Friedland was a microcosm of the mining industry that believed that profits were more valuable than protecting the environment. Scary to think that there were more Friedlands in the mining world.

Later, the reporter said in a newscast, "There is one word that describes when everything goes wrong at a mining site. And that one word is . . . Summitville."

Summitville was making history as one of the worst mining disasters in the United States. In the public meeting held in Capulin, Governor Romer had guaranteed that this Summitville disaster would not be repeated. Environmental groups, the mining industry, and the state were highly motivated to adopt major regulatory changes. On April 26, 1993, the Colorado State Legislature unanimously passed Senate Bill 247 that included "the requirement of environmental protection plans, for the reopening of mining operation permits, for the increasing of requirements for financial warranties, and for the creation of an emergency response system including the creation of an emergency response cash fund." Time would judge the effectiveness of these new environmental protection plans.

My frustrations with the bureaucrats continued. Our opinions were not taken seriously, just our participation to meet the requirements of Superfund. The end result was a clash of two cultures that no one addressed. No one tried to merge biological science with local knowledge.

Our group's anger about living with a dead river was never directly addressed. The state government made it easy to project our anger at them since they failed to thoroughly monitor the site. Unfortunately, our daily routines and needs had been intruded upon by someone else's negligence. And Dr. Harold—with his condescending arrogant attitude— re-victimized us and fueled our emotional fire. A complaint to the governor's office may have corrected the situation with a request that his future representative possess skills of collaboration and valued relationship-building. Before I knew it, I had justification for my resignation from the committee.

I telephoned Alice. "Hi, I have something to tell you. I've decided I don't want to serve anymore. I can't handle the four-hour meetings. I feel powerless with the state and the feds."

"No, don't quit. We need you."

"No, I've made up my mind. Life is too short. I'm out."

With a sense of relief, I hung up the phone.

However, several days later, the Black Madonna intervened with a dream:

A female voice said: "As you heal the river, you will also be healed. It is the community's involvement that will help rectify this environmental disaster. I will show you the way."

Like other auditory dreams, I avoided analyzing it; rather, I surrendered to the advice that the dream offered. I needed to be healed, but I was uncertain about how this would happen. The Black Madonna assured me that she would show me the way. I was grateful for her guidance. I did not have to decimate a mountain to find the Black Madonna's nuggets of gold and silver. They existed in my dream life and intuition. As a community we needed to forge ahead.

The dream reenergized me to continue participating in the Superfund process. The Alamosa River was a popular water hole where kids swam and tubed at the Lelo and the Numero Uno ditches. Someday, kids would continue generating memories of yanking fish out of the river and splashing and laughing in the water as they floated down the river in tubes. With the closest movie theater twenty-three miles away, the kids depended on the river for their recreation.

I was grateful that monies in the Superfund Trust Fund—taxes collected from the mining, oil, and gas industries—was available to cover expenses when the liable parties either are unable or refuse to be responsible for an environmental cleanup. Summitville Consolidated Mining Company had declared bankruptcy and left the financial responsibility for whomever had the money. The state of Colorado had limited resources, and our county government was even more strapped. The remediation fell on the shoulders of the federal EPA and the monies in the Superfund Trust Fund.

Unfortunately, in 1995, three years after Summitville was designated a Superfund site, Congress failed to renew the taxes collected from the mining, oil, and gas industries that funded the Superfund program. In the future, environmental disasters would require an act of Congress to pay for future cleanups. To be dependent on funding from Congress and their inability to work together was a depressing thought. In the future, the taxpayers would be held financially responsible in contrast to the prevailing principle, "polluters pay." Fortunately, this change did not affect the funding for Summitville.

Another component that complicated the situation was that Summitville was located in Rio Grande County whose county commissioners supported this mining venture. Unfortunately, the pollution flowed into the Alamosa River via Wightman Fork, which was located in neighboring Conejos County. People who had not participated in the decision-making process regarding the approval of the project were now involved in its remediation. It left another bitter taste in my mouth.

Around 1998, the local group became more confident, and our voices became stronger and louder. As a group, we wanted to write our own agenda rather than having the agenda handed to us. This laid the groundwork for the founding of an independent environmental organization. With seventy-five dollars in our budget, independent of any governmental agencies, and with the wealth of our voices and the freedom to share our traditional knowledge, Restore Our Alamosa River (ROAR) was born.

At the time, I was a board member of a charitable foundation. For our annual fundraiser, we decided to ask Robert F. Kennedy, Jr.—a proponent for environmental stewardship—be our featured speaker. He was also president of Waterkeeper® Alliance, an international environmental organization. I invited all the members of ROAR to attend the fundraiser, which gave us an opportunity to talk with Kennedy about Summitville.

"Apply for membership to the Waterkeeper Alliance. Tell us your story, and we'll let you know if you're accepted," Kennedy said.

"Why would you be interested in such a small town as ours? Granted, we often feel isolated, and being part of a larger organization would provide a lot of support," I said.

He smiled. "This is what we do. Please apply. This is our contact information."

We applied for membership and were accepted as the

Alamosa RIVERKEEPER® with the mission "to strive for a clean, functional river system which benefits the economic, ecological and recreational needs of the community." Legal experts had criticized local citizens for being lax in opposing the permitting required by Galactic Resources. Perhaps now, that criticism could be laid to rest.

As a member of the Waterkeeper Alliance, my eyes were forced open to the water quality deterioration that was plaguing other countries. Whether it was a river in Columbia, India, Mexico, Iraq, or Africa, rivers had evolved into cesspools of raw sewage, garbage, chemicals, and heavy metals. In turn, some of these same rivers were used for drinking and bathing purposes. Many countries lacked any governmental protection for their environment like we had in the United States. The Waterkeeper Alliance, in partnership with Three Rivers Waterkeeper, sponsored their annual conference in Pittsburgh, Pennsylvania. Riverkeepers from all over the world attended. One of the guest speakers was His Holiness the Gyalwang Drukpa, head of the Buddhist Drukpa Lineage, who later would cofound the Himalayan Glacier Waterkeeper. In his speech, His Holiness spoke about the need to take action, especially with climate change. Later, in partnership with Live to Love International and Waterkeeper Alliance, they launched the Himalayan Initiative to protect the waters of Ladakh and the Himalayas, the largest freshwater resource for nearly half the world's population. This was only one example of the great environmental work being done in the world. Thousands of courageous activists were improving the water quality in their bays, streams, and rivers, which inspired me to continue working to protect the Alamosa River.

At Summitville, the $15 million projected cost for the remediation continued to climb. Eventually the total cost would exceed $220 million. The federal and state governments were after Robert Friedland, CEO of Galactic Resources, to recover remediation costs at the mine site. I often imagined what my conversations with Friedland would sound like. "How dare you impose your negligence on my life and the lives of my children? How dare you destroy our fishery and our mountains, then you get exported to some third world country? You're probably polluting their water, too."

In 2000, the federal and state governments finally got their hands on Friedland. Under litigation captioned, "United States of America and State of Colorado vs. Robert M. Friedland, et al., CV 96-N1312 (D.Colo.)," the federal and state attorney generals recovered costs incurred to remediate the Summitville Superfund site under the authority of the Comprehensive Environmental Response, Compensation, and Liability Act (CERCLA) of 1980. The purpose of the act was "to restore, replace or acquire the equivalent of the natural resources damaged" by the hazardous substances released from the Summitville mine.

In 2001, I received a telephone call from the state attorney general's office. He explained that a natural damage resource settlement against Friedland was almost complete.

"Would you be willing to give Friedland a tour of the Alamosa River watershed, so he can actually see the impacted area?"

"Who?"

"Robert Friedland."

I almost dropped the telephone.

"The negotiations are in a delicate stage. All you have to do is show Friedland and his attorney the Alamosa River," he said.

"Okay." I thought I could face our enemy.

"I'll be calling with details."

Later, I asked myself whether I could meet this man when I had so much anger toward him. How could he walk away and leave such devastation for the United States, for Colorado, and for the ranchers, farmers, and my family who were dependent on this river?

Again, I needed another heart-to-heart with the Black Madonna. My fury toward Friedland was as hot as simmering coals, but I refused to have my anger sabotage this important meeting. The only way I could be civil was by meditating every day. In the Madonna's maternal love, I prayed the rosary and absorbed her peace, love, and determination. When my anger popped up, I acknowledged it until it naturally subsided. Most likely, my emotions would remain with me, but not enough to undermine our goals. This settlement was important. I had to do everything in my power—and in the Madonna's—to make Friedland accountable for his negligence.

Weeks later, I met Friedland and his attorney at our local airport. Introductions were as warm as a subzero morning in the Valley. Friedland was of medium height, courteous, but cautious. When I dropped a paper in the car, he automatically picked it up. However, below the surface, I felt that, at any time, there was an alligator ready to snap.

I drove Friedland through the Alamosa River watershed. I parked the car by the Alamosa River. Friedland said, "The EPA caused this mess at Summitville; it was their fault."

Hmm, his logic was not making sense. I continued to listen as Friedland tried to absolve himself from any responsibility. Inwardly, I countered, *If you hadn't discharged contaminated water over the land that eventually reached the Alamosa River, the EPA wouldn't have been forced to take over the operations at Summitville.*

Only later did I understand Friedland's anger at the EPA. In the 1990's, the EPA had received anonymous telephone calls reporting discharges without permits at the mine site. After the EPA inspected the area, they informed the state of Colorado that either the state or EPA needed to take enforcement action. The state agreed to take action, but when Galactic Resources abandoned the mine, the EPA eventually had to recover the site.

As I drove Friedland and his attorney through the watershed, I was constantly on edge. Anything could make me snap. I thought if I said too much, one of us would be floating like the fish down the river.

Friedland had satisfied the requirement to visit the watershed. A few hours later, I drove him and his attorney, who had hardly said a word and had only served as a witness, to their private plane. Friedland wanted to meet in Denver to discuss other funding resources for the community center. Of course, I was intrigued by his proposal. Maybe the center could receive some financial compensation. Sometimes I surprised myself with the degree of my naiveté. I should have known better.

A few days later, with trepidation, I met Friedland at the bar at the Westin Hotel in Denver. He was preparing to leave on an afternoon flight. The waiter served me a glass of wine, when the alligator snapped. "How do you think it feels to be called an environmental rapist?" Friedland yelled.

I was speechless. I had referred to him as an environmental rapist to anyone who would listen, which included eager newspaper reporters, foreigners, locals, and agency people. I could not hold back my colorful opinions of him.

Friedland beat me to the punch. He opened the door leading out of the bar, whipped around, and said, "You might think about working out more."

He was gone before I could respond. Perhaps I could have thrown the wine glass at him and yelled, "Well, if I didn't have to attend so many draining meetings to remediate all the damage you caused, maybe I could exercise more."

Friedland had a habit of vanishing when the heat got too hot. Unfortunately, he did not take the Summitville disaster with him. No, he left the mess with hundreds of people who would work for decades on the aftermath of *his* environmental irresponsibility. None of his pitiful insults could be as severe as being labeled an environmental rapist. No surprise, not even a penny was offered for the community center.

Driving home, I reflected on Friedland's insult. I could have felt hurt, but his words were powerless. I remembered my dream when the female voice said, *as you heal the river, you will also be healed. It is the community's involvement that will help rectify this environmental disaster. I will show you the way.*

I had worked on this dream, but as usual, symbols have layers of meaning. The Black Madonna, through my dreams and in meditation, showed me the way by transmuting my ignorance on environmental degradation into knowledge and stewardship. I had garnered my environmental awareness through participation in meetings with the Superfund process and through cofounding an environmental organization. Like a water lily, I grew in the dark muck—the earthen bottom of my ignorance and vulnerability—which forced me to learn about water quality and water quantity issues, the corrosiveness of heavy metals, and legislation like the Clean Water Act. In meditation, I was energized to continue learning, and I was propelled to act upon my insights and ideas. My new environmental consciousness had forever empowered me. Friedland's desperate attempt to get me to Denver and hurt my feelings failed.

Through the natural resource damage settlement, Friedland paid $28.5 million with $5 million designated for the Alamosa River watershed to restore it to conditions prior to the Summitville disaster.

If someone had asked me, "How do you restore a polluted river?"

I would have said, "With money, people, and luck."

The Alamosa River Watershed Restoration Master Plan and Environmental Assessment, funded by the settlement monies, was completed in 2005. The master plan helped prioritize the needs of the watershed. An instream flow in the river, embankment stabilization, and other projects were designated as priorities. Alamosa Riverkeeper applied for funding for an instream flow project that would extend the flows in the river when the irrigation season was completed. These extended flows would help develop a fishery that had been destroyed, would restore the habitat, and would help regenerate the aquifer that had been depleted as result of a multi-year drought.

Funding was essential, but people working together was equally important. Extending flows in the river was a new concept. Even some of the trustees for the natural resource damage settlement had their doubts whether we could really find the water and secure its storage.

People who participated in the public meetings said:

"This has never been done before."

"You won't be able to buy the water that you need."

"The river was only meant for irrigation."

I responded, "You're right. We've never had an instream flow on the Alamosa River. But you're leading the way. This is a once-in-a-lifetime opportunity for our watershed to be restored. Don't you love fishing? There's nothing like that sudden pull on your fishing pole, right? No doubt, irrigation is vital for our economy, but sharing water for a fishery is possible."

Other issues that had to be dealt with were feuds between people that dated back 100 years. I stressed that people had to work together and that animosity was not going to benefit the project. Those who refused to sit at the table would be left in the dust. Some remained sitting, and others left.

Then President Obama's American Recovery and Reinvestment Act provided stimulus monies. We were fortunate to have politicians who supported funding for a $19 million water treatment plant at the headwaters of the Alamosa River. The new water treatment plant significantly improved the water quality in the river. Twenty years after Summitville was declared a Superfund site, the water in the Alamosa River was clean enough to sustain a fishery. The fish were annually stocked in Terrace Reservoir, and, upon the state's testing, the fish could be eaten. And once again, I enjoyed panfried trout caught in the river.

I heard from anglers:

"I caught a fourteen-inch rainbow just below Terrace."

"I caught fish at the Alamosa Campground. I've never caught fish there before."

Soon I heard these holy words: "The fish are spawning below Terrace."

Cleaner water was essential for the recovery of the river and its fishery. We as a community refused to remain victims of one of the worst mining disasters in the United States.

And what about our buddy Friedland? I was confident that he was not counting copper pennies. Forbes Magazine listed Friedland as a billionaire with offices headquartered in Singapore and mining operations in Guayana and other places. He owned South American Goldfields that reportedly dumped over a billion gallons of cyanide-laced tailings into two Guayana rivers. *Again* he resigned, avoiding any financial responsibility.

Chapter Thirteen

Santo Niño de Atocha

As well as being an environmental activist, I facilitated two groups: the Celebration and Creativity of the Crone and Working with Dreams. Diane, a dream group participant, recruited me to co-facilitate a Crone workshop. I provided the background on the Feminine, and she used polymer clay to help the participants create their Crone who captured their unique wisdom.

My presentation from a Jungian perspective included the three complementary aspects of the Feminine in both women and men: the Virgin, sometimes referred to as the Maiden; the Mother; and the Crone.

The aspect of my Virgin emerged when I was animated, when I was well-connected to my emotions, and when I sparkled with hope and possibilities. Being an observer of life was not an option when I could fully engage in the world's excitement and challenges.

The Mother exemplifies nurturing, loving, and compassion.

I found myself nurturing children, my own and others, through the center's tutoring program, summer day camp, and folkloric dance troupe. I identified with everyone. I witnessed the pain and joy of others, even though at times it was difficult to share in their sufferings.

One time while visiting Seattle, Andrea and I flagged down a cab. A holy card that had a picture of the Virgin Mary and Child was sitting on the console. Andrea leaned over, "Do you pray to Our Lady?"

"Oh yes, she and I have a history," said the driver who looked Persian.

Don't we all, I thought to myself.

"She is my mother and the mother of everyone. So that makes all of us brothers and sisters."

Andrea and I looked at each other and smiled. The cab driver was absolutely right. The Black Madonna was our universal mother, and we were all connected through her presence in all our psyches.

Another aspect of the Feminine is the Crone, who carries wisdom garnered by lessons of living, such as surviving illnesses, coping with deaths of loved ones, and overcoming emotional and physical wounds. Within time, these lessons are transformed into pearls of wisdom. After all, natural pearls are formed when an irritant, like a piece of sand, works its way into a shell. As a defense mechanism, a fluid, referred to as a nacre, is used to coat the irritant. Layer upon layer of nacre is deposited until a lustrous pearl is formed. Like a typical Crone, I had gathered my pearls of wisdom by learning compassion when I was diagnosed with Bell's Palsy. My endometriosis taught me to be empathic with other women who suffer through gynecological problems. Through my divorce I learned that communication was a form of love and that it was imperative in building a marriage, even if it required that we fought and, instead of drinking coffee, we needed to throw the coffee cups on the floor to keep us awake or conscious about our feelings. And my community and environmental work taught me how essential listening with the heart, collaboration, and patience were.

In the American culture, the Crone sometimes has to push others aside to find a seat at the table. She gladly does this, for she is anxious to share her strong rich voice that emanates from her experiences. She solidly speaks from her emotions and from her body that is infused with wisdom. Sometimes, it is hard to listen to her blunt honesty, but at the same time her words are refreshingly real. She does not seek admiration, for she is content wearing her pearls of strength created from her struggles. The Crone sees things the way they are and has the means to create change. People are drawn to the Crone's authenticity as if she were an apple pie right out of the oven, bubbling with cinnamon and sugar.

The patriarchy, in my case the "water buffalos," older

men who own and control water rights, found my attitude threatening because I was able to express my perspective. My Crone had the ability to see straight through their egos, which once forced me to walk out of a meeting. I had become the focal point, the person who was blocking their control of the project's money. Alamosa Riverkeeper was specifically asked to oversee the money by being the project manager. These men were like bull dogs trying to tear me apart. Others in the room supported me, but nothing was going to stop their attack. I picked up my purse, put on my coat, and walked out of the room.

As I was walking to my car, a woman was following me. She said, "You know this is about your being a woman. Don't take it personally. I've experienced this type of behavior in my life." I showed my appreciation for her support by giving her a big hug.

Interestingly, on the other hand, there were younger men who owned lots of water rights, who were partners with Alamosa Riverkeeper, and who taught me about water law. They served as my mentors in the water world. I was not a threat to them. They realized that working together we could accomplish so much more than working against each other. Hopefully these men are the future generation of "water buffalos" who know that the key to success is their ability to form partnerships and know how to collaborate.

The next morning, I received telephone calls from people who thanked me for my leadership and offered their support. Even one of my attackers apologized for his misbehavior.

In the Crone workshops, I stressed that, in Western culture, outer beauty, youth, and material possessions were sometimes valued more than the lessons offered from the aging process. Some people thirst for the fountain of youth, which was evident in some American cities where more plastic surgeons were employed than pediatricians. Without a strong core of love and compassion, the value of beauty and wealth can disappear as fast as a sandcastle at high tide.

Some women in the Crone workshop found it difficult to bring their pearls of wisdom from the basements of their psyches, brush off the cobwebs, and place them around their necks where they could be reminded of their inner beauty and strength. At times, their negative connotation of the Crone was inhibiting them.

When I searched for the Crone's story in the dictionary, I read, "A withered, witchlike old woman [Middle English, Middle Dutch *old ewe, dead body*; old North French *carrion*; Vulgar Latin *flesh*]." The Crone's wisdom lies deep in the cells of her body. Sometimes, aging leaves wrinkles and scars that are difficult to look at. But these wrinkles and their stories help the women's psyches to develop them into the people they were meant to be.

My goal was to live from these three aspects of the Feminine by listening to my emotions, loving freely with compassion for myself and for others, and trusting life's switchbacks that offer lessons along the way.

In 1996, I was invited to speak about the Black Madonna at a women's conference and to facilitate a breakout session in "How to Work with Dreams." After the presentation, Kay and Kathy approached me and asked if I would facilitate a dream group. I said "yes," and, two decades later, they and others are still listening to their dream symbols. The longevity of the group speaks to the women's commitment and dedication to their personal growth. Knowing that there was support and a physical space where they could listen and reflect on their dreams was invaluable, especially in the hustle-bustle of the American lifestyle. The dreamers helped me to stay committed to my dreams as well.

Even though I had been working with my dreams for over thirty years, I knew that writing my dreams required discipline. It was difficult to get up in the middle of the night and scribble a dream in my notebook. But if I lacked this discipline, most likely I would lose the dream's message. I found that the more hectic and stressful my life was, the less likely I was able to remember the dream. Usually, I meditated and worked on dreams in the living room, sitting in a comfortable chair that faced the icon of the Black Madonna. When I visited big cities like Seattle, I wondered how people could secure a meditative place, a refuge, among the tall skyscrapers and walls of concrete. But I was hopeful that they could secure a quiet space in their home, in a church, or by sitting next to a stream.

Belonging to a group or working with a dream partner definitely helped the dreamers to stay disciplined and committed to self-reflection, which was required for a relationship with the Feminine. The size of a group ranged from two to five people. Depending on the number of participants, two to three hours were allowed so that everyone had time to work on their dream. I expected that their dream was already written in their journal *exactly* how they had dreamt it. Each person took a turn sharing usually one dream. The golden rule was that the dreamer's interpretation was the most valuable. After years of sharing intimate details of our lives in the dream group, many times we had pre-holiday gatherings or trips, especially before Christmas.

One Christmas week, I was busy wrapping gifts and filling paper sacks with sand and a candle for the *luminarias* when a profound dream made me pause.

December 23, 2004

I'm polishing the pews at the church. I turn to look at the alcove with a statue of the Blessed Virgin Mary.

To my surprise, instead of seeing a statue of Mary, a darling boy is sitting on a wooden chair with a feathered cap on top of his long curly hair.

He's wearing a blue robe that is covered with a white lace collar and a brown furry cape. In his left hand he holds a small woven basket.

And in his right hand, he's holding a water gourd suspended from a pilgrim's staff.

I refrained from analyzing this spiritual dream. Rather, I remained in the experience that was offered by the dream. I wanted to grab this precious child and sit him on my lap. I imagined playing with the feather on his cap, rubbing the fur on his cape, and caressing his soft face. This darling child was such a novelty. Who was he anyway? Days later, I realized that I had seen another picture of him, but where? When I found the book, there he was: Santo Niño de Atocha, the Christ Child. I continued reading his history.

The legend of Santo Niño began in Atocha, Spain. Atocha is located outside of Madrid where, during the thirteenth century, the city was ruled by Muslims. During those tumultuous times, many Christians were imprisoned and could only be fed by children under the age of twelve and from their own families. But many of the prisoners were without kids and were left to starve.

The women of Atocha began praying to Our Lady of Atocha (the Blessed Virgin Mary) and requested that her son, Jesus, help them. Before long, the prisoners were visited by a Spanish pilgrim child who shared water from his gourd and bread from his basket. At the same time, the child Jesus on the statue of Our Lady of Atocha was wearing tattered, dusty shoes. The villagers were convinced that it was Jesus visiting these prisoners.

I often wondered why this image of Santo Niño replaced the statue of Mary in my dream. Certainly, in Christianity, Jesus Christ brought a radical message in violent Roman times of "loving one another as I have loved you." At the time of this dream, I was feeling frustrated with a new order of priests who were serving at my Catholic Church. At first, I welcomed them into our parish by inviting them to dinner. But as time passed, their extreme dogma and judgmental attitude about non-Catholics and one's sexual orientation were offensive to me, especially when I knew that the Black Madonna loved everyone—Catholic, non-Catholic, atheist, Jew, Muslim—you name it, and she loves them. I tried to tolerate their Sunday homilies that promoted discrimination and condemnation of others who were different than they. Oftentimes, I walked out during their homilies. I tried discussing these issues with the priests, but they rarely budged from their position. On the other hand, I was reassured by the parishioners' strong faith whose forefathers (and mothers) built this church. They were examples of kindness and hospitality.

My dream was a reminder of Jesus's child-like love for me. When I looked for the statue of the Virgin Mary, instead of finding her, I found her son, Santo Niño. How could I continue feeling frustrated after seeing this precious child who showed me so much hope?

Psychologically, my dream indicated that it was the child's spontaneity, imagination, and acceptance that brought hope to Spain centuries ago, and he continues to feed me and others who are searching for freedom of the human soul. The Christ Child, or the creative spark of the Feminine, continues to be drawn to victims of addiction and violence, to refugees who are displaced and who are searching for a home, and even to rivers that are poisoned and are unable to sustain aquatic life!

Santo Niño reminded me of when the Black Madonna said, "I'm going to take Marissa," the child in my psyche who lives in the world of feelings and imagination. My biological mother was quiet in her love for me, although she completely provided food and shelter to satisfy my physical needs. But emotionally she was absent because she was raised in an alcoholic and abusive family where, as a child, out of desperation, she had abandoned her feelings. I understood, because I found it difficult to express my feelings, too. I had accepted Mom, especially when she cooked those soft buttery tortillas. I loved Mom for what she was capable of giving me rather than being resentful for what she was unable to provide me.

So, when I experienced the Black Madonna's divine maternal love, I learned all over again how to listen to my feelings. According to one of my auditory dreams, *the Divine*

Mother is a manifestation of God. If the Divine Mother is an aspect of God, then her motherly love is infinite and brings healing to the most extreme situations of abandonment.

In my vision in Einsiedeln, I never saw the Black Madonna's face. It was hidden by a monk-like hood. Yet, when she embraced me, I intuitively knew that she was the Black Madonna. Her source of love was boundless and infinite. A face would have set limitations with an illusion of individuality. On the contrary, the Black Madonna is a universal archetype found in the psyche of *all* men and women.

I reflected: *When I used the Feminine principle in my everyday life, did I create a space for her consciousness or awareness? Did I give form to the formless when I worked collaboratively on community and environmental projects, or when I showed compassion to another person?* With this thought, I felt a profound responsibility coupled with a feeling of unworthiness. In my humility, I was able to step up and be an advocate for the environment, learn about water quantity and water quality issues, and learn about community development and fundraising. Perhaps other men and women can find the Feminine principles of compassion, intuition, collaboration, honoring personal relationships, and protecting the earth helpful when they think about how they want to improve their lives and how they want to change the world.

Epilogue

In the gym at the community center, we were busy setting up tables and chairs for a fundraiser. Upon our acceptance into the Waterkeeper Alliance, Robert F. Kennedy, Jr., president, was launching our new program and helping us raise money. We had planned a big fiesta with music and food. Pee Wee wrestlers were practicing now on the other side of the gym. I was getting ready to leave when a little boy came racing toward me. Before I could react, he jumped into my arms and clasped his warm pudgy legs around my waist. I asked, "What's your name?"

"Johnny."

I paused and looked into his Swiss chocolate eyes. "So glad to meet you, Niño."

He grinned with joy then jumped out of my arms as fast as he had jumped into them. He ran with his pals across the gym floor and leapt onto the wrestling mats. My heartstrings were vibrating when a nostalgic feeling came over me. I was transported back to a time when the Black Madonna had first embraced the child within me so many years ago.

ભ   ભ   ભ

SUGGESTED READING

Andrews, Ted, *Animal-Speak: The Spiritual & Magical Powers of Creatures Great & Small*. St. Paul: Llewellyn Publications, 1998.

Begg, Ean, *The Cult of the Black Virgin*, Wilmette: Chiron Publications, 2006.

Brennan, Barbara Ann, *Hands of Light: A Guide to Healing Through the Human Energy Field*. New York: Bantam Books, 1987.

Chödrön, Pema, *How to Meditate: A Practical Guide to Making Friends with Your Mind*. Boulder: Sounds True, 2013.

Edited and Translated by Francisco A. Lomelí and Clark A. Colahan, *Defying the Inquisition in Colonial New Mexico: Miguel de Quintana's Life and Writings*. Albuquerque: University of New Mexico Press, 2006.

Estés, Pinkola Clarissa, *Women Who Run With the Wolves: Myth and Studies of the Wild Women Archetype*. New York: Random House, Inc., 1995

Illuminations of Hildegard of Bingen. Text by Hildegard of Bingen with commentary by Matthew Fox. Santa Fe: Bear & Company, 1985.

Gustafson, Fred, *The Black Madonna of Einsiedeln, An Ancient Image for Our Present Time*. Einsiedeln: Daimon Verlag, 2009.

Johnson, Robert A., *Inner Work: Using Dreams & Active Imagination for Personal Growth*. New York: HarperCollins, 2009.

Johnston, Francis, *The Wonder of Guadalupe*. Mexico: Editoral Verdad Y Vida, 1981.

Judith, Anodea, *Wheels of Life: Users Guide to the Chakra System*, St. Paul: Llewellyn Publications, 1999.

Jung, Carl G. *Archetypes of the Collective Unconscious, 9 C. W., Part I*. New York: Pantheon Books, 1959.

Kennedy, Robert F., Jr., *Crimes Against Nature*, New York: Harper-Collins Publishers Inc., 2004.

Le Mee, Katharine. *Chant: The Origins, Form, Practice, and Healing Power of Gregorian Chant*. New York: Bell Tower, 1994.

Lockhart, Russell A. and Hillman, James, et al. *Soul and Money*. Dallas: Spring Publications, Inc., 1982.

Luke, Helen M. *Woman, Earth, and Spirit: The Feminine in Symbol and Myth*. New York: Crossroad, 1981.

Merton, Thomas. *Thoughts in Solitude*. Boston: Shambhala, 1993.

Netboy, Anthony. *The Columbia River Salmon and Steelhead Trout: Their Fight for Survival*. Seattle: University of Washington Press, 1980.

Ouspensky, Leonid and Lossky, Vladimir. *The Meaning of Icons*. New York: St. Vladimir's Seminary Press, 1989.

Smith, David P. *Ouray: Chief of the Utes*. Ridgway: Wayfinder Press, 1990.

The Collected Works of St. John of the Cross. Translated by Kieran Kavanaugh, and Otilio Rodriguez. Washington, DC., ICS Publications, 1991.

The Sacred Heritage: The Influence of Shamanism on Analytical Psychology. Edited by Donald F. Sandner & Steven H. Wong. New York, London: Routledge, 1997.

Tushar, Olibama Lopez, *The People of El Valle: A History of the Spanish Settlers in the San Luis Valley*. Pueblo: El Escritorio, 2007.

Woodman, Marion and Dickson, Elinor. *Dancing in the Flames: The Dark Goddess in the Transformation of Consciousness*. Boston & London, Shambhala, 1997.

www.cindymmedina.com

About the Author

Ms. Medina has devoted her life to the emergence of the Feminine in the lives of women and men. She has integrated the Feminine perspective in her psychotherapeutic practice, and through community development with a focus on environmental justice.

After graduating from Colorado State University with a BS in psychology and earning a Master's degree in Counseling from Arizona State University, Ms. Medina trained in Process-oriented Psychology, with an emphasis in Jungian Psychology, in Zurich, Switzerland. As the Alamosa Riverkeeper, she received the David Getches Flowing Waters Award for improving environmental water resources and recreational values in the Alamosa River through her efforts in collaboration, innovation and inspiration.

Cindy treasures solitude that is often interrupted by owls hooting from the cottonwood trees, by coyotes howling from the Alamosa River, and by irrigation water flowing through the *acequia* (dirt ditch).